JEREMIAH
BIBLE STUDY SERIES

1 & 2 PETER

THE WAY TO ENDURE THROUGH TRIALS

DR. DAVID JEREMIAH

Prepared by Peachtree Publishing Services

HarperChristian
Resources

1 & 2 Peter
Jeremiah Bible Study Series

© 2022 by Dr. David Jeremiah

Requests for information should be addressed to:
HarperChristian Resources, 3900 Sparks Dr. SE, Grand Rapids, Michigan 49546

ISBN 978-0-310-09182-0 (softcover)
ISBN 978-0-310-09183-7 (ebook)

HarperChristian Resources titles may be purchased in bulk for church, business, fundraising,
or ministry use. For information, please email ResourceSpecialist@ChurchSource.com.

Produced with the assistance of Peachtree Publishing Services (www.PeachtreePublishingServices.
com). Project staff includes Christopher D. Hudson and Randy Southern.

First Printing April 2022 / Printed in the United States of America

CONTENTS

INTRODUCTION TO
The Letters of 1 & 2 Peter

"Sanctify the Lord God in your hearts, and always be ready to give a defense to everyone who asks you a reason for the hope that is in you" (1 Peter 3:15–16). The disciple Peter, who penned these words, had witnessed the words, works, and wonders of the man he called the Messiah. He had seen not only the anguish that others had inflicted on Christ but also the suffering that his own denials had caused his Savior and friend. But Peter had also witnessed the resurrection of Jesus . . . and that had changed *everything*. Ever since that time, Peter had been "ready to give a defense" to anyone who asked about Jesus and how to receive salvation. He was thus uniquely qualified to remind first-century believers about the hope they had received through Christ, their mission to the world, and how to endure through sufferings.

1 PETER

Author and Date

The writer of this letter identifies himself as "Peter, an apostle of Jesus Christ" (1:1) and "a witness of the sufferings of Christ" (5:1). His personal references to first-century church leaders such as "Silvanus [Silas], our faithful brother" and "[John] Mark my son" (5:12–13), in addition to his identification with his audience and the sufferings of Christ, all support the case that the letter was written by the disciple Peter. Furthermore, early church fathers such as Irenaeus (c. AD 130–202) recognized Peter as the author—though the stylistic eloquence of the wording indicates that it was likely penned by a person fluent in Greek (probably Silas). Peter likely wrote or dictated the letter around AD 64, just a few years before his execution. Church tradition held that Peter spent his last years ministering in Rome, and a reference in the letter to Rome as "Babylon" (5:13), indicate that it was likely the place of composition.

Background and Setting

Peter addresses his letter to "the pilgrims of the Dispersion in Pontus, Galatia, Cappadocia, Asia, and Bithynia" (1:1), which comprise the northern region of Asia Minor (modern-day Turkey). This group certainly includes Jewish believers who had fled Jerusalem after the martyrdom of Stephen and the outbreak of persecution (see Acts 8:1). But Peter's references to his readers' former way of living (see 1 Peter 1:14–15, 18, 22; 4:1–5) indicates that his audience was also comprised of Gentile believers from various races and ethnic backgrounds. These believers had been "dispersed" from their societies as a result of the intensifying persecutions against the growing Christian movement by Roman authorities in the first century. Peter wrote to provide all these believers with hope in the midst of their trials and to answer their questions about Jesus' return, what He wanted from them in the meantime, and their responsibilities as citizens, workers, and spouses. Peter shares the wisdom he gained at the feet of Jesus Himself.

Key Themes

Several themes are prominent in the letter of 1 Peter. The first is that *believers in Christ are called to a life of holiness* (see 1 Peter 1:2–25). The believers to whom Peter was writing were being pressured to adapt to Roman culture and to adopt Roman practices. In response to that pressure, Peter challenges them to lean into God's grace and cultivate a holy life. In this way, they would serve as living examples of God's holiness to an unholy world.

A second theme is that *believers in Christ are called to submit to authority* (see 2:13–3:12). Peter recognizes that God's design for human systems includes "horizontal" relationships (personal interactions among people in a society) and also "vertical" relationships (the hierarchy at work in government, business, and the family). Believers must take their respective place in these chains of command and submit to those God has placed over them—not because they were inferior to those individuals but because the Lord required it of them.

A third theme is that *believers in Christ are called to endure in trials* (see 3:13–5:11). During the reign of Emperor Nero, Christians became a persecuted minority in the Roman Empire. Understandably, many new believers were experiencing doubt and discouragement in the midst of their suffering. So, Peter provides guidance on how they can endure—looking to the suffering that Christ endured for their sake as an example.

2 PETER

Author and Date

The writer of this letter identifies himself as "Simon Peter" (1:1) and states that he was an eyewitness to events in Jesus' life (see 1:16–18). However, the language used, along with its close association to the letter of Jude, caused some in the early church to doubt the disciple Peter actually wrote it. The debate continued into the fourth century, when the church finally recognized it to be authentic and received it into the New Testament canon. Given Peter's acknowledgement in his first letter that he was working through a scribe (see 1 Peter 5:12), it is reasonable to conclude that he dictated this letter as well through a scribe, which would account for the discrepancies in style and tone between the two letters. Assuming Peter is the author, it was likely written from Rome before his death c. AD 64–68.

Background and Setting

Peter addresses his second letter to "those who have obtained . . . precious faith with us by the righteousness of our God and Savior Jesus Christ"

(2 Peter 1:1). While this designation makes it impossible to conclude the intended recipients with any certainty, references in the letter point to a group of believers located in Greece or Asia Minor, where the apostle Paul's letters had circulated (see 3:15–16). If this is correct, the audience would thus be primarily Gentile believers who were living in a Roman society that was generally opposed to the message of the gospel. Peter encourages these believers to pursue a godly lifestyle in spite of the culture around them, reject false teachings opposed to the gospel, and again endure in trials.

Key Themes

Several key themes are prominent in the letter of 2 Peter. The first theme is that *believers in Christ should pursue God's truth* (see 2 Peter 1:3–18). Peter reminds his readers that he was an eyewitness to the ministry of the One who called Himself "the way, the truth, and the life" (John 14:6). He uses the word *knowledge* four times in his opening chapter alone (see 1:3, 5, 6, 8) to urge his readers to pursue an intimate interaction with the truths of God. He wants them to apply God's truths to their daily lives so they can mature in their faith.

A second theme is that *believers in Christ must adhere to the message of the gospel* (see 2:1–22). False teachers were a continual problem in the early church because they made convincing arguments that sounded rational to their listeners but were contrary to the gospel. Many believers were led astray by these false teachings and wandered from God's truth. Peter doesn't go into detail about the nature of the false teaching that he is addressing, but he implores believers to embrace the message of the gospel they received from the true apostles.

A third theme is that *believers in Christ can be assured that Jesus will return* (see 3:1–13). Peter warns the believers that "scoffers" would come into their congregations and proclaim that Jesus had failed to deliver on his promise of returning to this earth. These individuals would point out that "all things continue as they were from the beginning of creation" (3:4). Peter assures his readers that any delay on Christ's return is not a failure on God's part to deliver on His promises. Rather, God is giving humanity time so that all who are willing with "come to repentance" (3:9) and put their faith in Christ.

KEY APPLICATIONS

Peter offers guidance to all followers of Christ on how to navigate the challenges and trials of this life. Although we live on this earth, and seek to be productive members of society, we have to always remember that we are really just "pilgrims" passing through on our way to heaven. As citizens of God's kingdom who live on foreign turf, we can expect to be harassed from time to time. We can also expect there will be some individuals who will challenge our beliefs and faith in Christ and try to lead us to accept the world's standard of living. Peter's message is to stay strong and keep our focus on God's truth. We must remember God's promises, ponder them, claim them, pray them back to the Lord, and then act on what He calls us to do.

A LIVING HOPE

1 Peter 1:1–12

GETTING STARTED

What comes to your mind when you picture the words *hope* and *joy*?

_____

_____

_____

_____

_____

_____

_____

_____

_____

_____

_____

_____

SETTING THE STAGE

Peter's first letter is written to believers in Christ who were scattered throughout five different regions of the Roman Empire. Individuals from these same regions are mentioned in the book of Acts as being present on the Day of Pentecost when the Holy Spirit fell on those gathered in the upper room (see Acts 2:1–13). On that day, people heard the gospel in their own language and received God's salvation. In 1 Peter, we learn what happened next.

These new believers went back to their own communities to live out the faith that they had found in Christ. However, they quickly discovered that they were now in the minority. Even worse, they found that the former system of the world to which they used to belong was now often hostile toward them. In his letter, Peter refers to them as being "grieved by various trials" (1:6) and to their situation as a "fiery trial" (4:12). They were living in a culture that did not know them, did not accept them, did not understand them, and did not like them.

Peter wanted to help. He wanted to encourage these believers by "exhorting and testifying that this is the true grace of God in which you stand" (5:12. The word *exhort* means to comfort. *Testify* means to share a personal experience. So, Peter is saying, "I want to tell you what God says about His grace and how I have experienced that grace in my own life."

In this opening section of his letter, Peter acknowledges the believers' bleak situation but asks them to remember that they are God's elect and He is going to take care of them. This truth also applies to us as we read these words from Peter. His "good news for bad times" still has the power to encourage us when we are down, strengthen us when we are weak, help us when we reach the limits of our power, motivate us when things look bleak, and send us on our way rejoicing—no matter how difficult things in this life may be.

Exploring the Text

Grace and Peace Be Multiplied (1 Peter 1:1–5)

¹ Peter, an apostle of Jesus Christ,

To the pilgrims of the Dispersion in Pontus, Galatia, Cappadocia, Asia, and Bithynia, ² elect according to the foreknowledge of God the

Father, in sanctification of the Spirit, for obedience and sprinkling of the blood of Jesus Christ:

Grace to you and peace be multiplied.

[3] Blessed be the God and Father of our Lord Jesus Christ, who according to His abundant mercy has begotten us again to a living hope through the resurrection of Jesus Christ from the dead, [4] to an inheritance incorruptible and undefiled and that does not fade away, reserved in heaven for you, [5] who are kept by the power of God through faith for salvation ready to be revealed in the last time.

---

1. Peter designates the recipients of his letter as pilgrims who have dispersed to regions throughout the Roman Empire. The term *pilgrim* refers to temporary residents of a foreign land who live with a constant awareness of their true home. How does this awareness give hope to the Christian pilgrims who are experiencing trials and suffering (see verses 1–2)?

2. Peter recognizes that his readers have been *dispersed* to many different lands due to the persecution that was being inflicted on them by the governing authorities. He has also endured such persecution, but he is still able to express his praise to God. What hope does he say that believers have in spite of their present circumstances (see verses 3–5)?

A Heavenly Inheritance (1 Peter 1:6–12)

⁶ In this you greatly rejoice, though now for a little while, if need be, you have been grieved by various trials, ⁷ that the genuineness of your faith, being much more precious than gold that perishes, though it is tested by fire, may be found to praise, honor, and glory at the revelation of Jesus Christ, ⁸ whom having not seen you love. Though now you do not see Him, yet believing, you rejoice with joy inexpressible and full of glory, ⁹ receiving the end of your faith—the salvation of your souls.

¹⁰ Of this salvation the prophets have inquired and searched carefully, who prophesied of the grace that would come to you, ¹¹ searching what, or what manner of time, the Spirit of Christ who was in them was indicating when He testified beforehand the sufferings of Christ and the glories that would follow. ¹² To them it was revealed that, not to themselves, but to us they were ministering

the things which now have been reported to you through those who have preached the gospel to you by the Holy Spirit sent from heaven—things which angels desire to look into.

---

3. Peter wants his readers to understand that the trials they are facing will ultimately serve a purpose. Much as a metalworker refines ore in a fire to burn off the impurities, so the fires of their lives are refining them into something greater. What does Peter say this refining process will yield? For what reason can they rejoice in spite of trials (see verses 6–9)?

_____

_____

_____

_____

_____

4. Peter draws on the example of the Old Testament prophets to reveal another reason why believers can rejoice. What does he say the prophets received from God? What have believers in Christ received? Why should this give them hope (see verses 10–12)?

_____

_____

_____

_____

_____

_____

GOING DEEPER

The trials that Peter's readers were facing appear to have arisen out of the tension between their faith in Christ and the values of the culture around them. In some cases, these trials were severe and included not only exclusion from society but also imprisonment and physical harm. Even so, Peter encourages these believers to rejoice in trials, know their persecution is arising out of their identification with the risen Christ. In Paul's letter to the church in Rome, we find a similar call for the believers to rejoice in spite of their circumstances. Joy is seen not as a fleeting feeling borne out of the moment but as a lifestyle of gratitude and thankfulness to God for providing the gift of an eternal security that transcends the turmoil of this world.

Faith Triumphs in Trouble (Romans 5:1–5)

¹ Therefore, having been justified by faith, we have peace with God through our Lord Jesus Christ, ² through whom also we have access by faith into this grace in which we stand, and rejoice in hope of the glory of God. ³ And not only that, but we also glory in tribulations, knowing that tribulation produces perseverance; ⁴ and perseverance, character; and character, hope. ⁵ Now hope does not disappoint, because the love of God has been poured out in our hearts by the Holy Spirit who was given to us.

5. The fact that we are justified by faith completely changes our relationship with God. What does Paul say we secure through Christ? What is it about this new relationship and standing before God that should give us hope in this life (see verses 1–2)?

----

6. Paul notes that hope is not something that magically appears in our lives but is forged through the fires of trial. It is the end result of a process of enduring through tribulations, which produces perseverance, which in turn produces character, which then leads to hope. How can we be sure this our hard-earned hope will not disappoint us (see verses 3–5)?

_____

_____

_____

_____

_____

_____

_____

From Suffering to Glory (Romans 8:18–25)

[18] For I consider that the sufferings of this present time are not worthy to be compared with the glory which shall be revealed in us. [19] For the earnest expectation of the creation eagerly waits for the revealing of the sons of God. [20] For the creation was subjected to futility, not willingly, but because of Him who subjected it in hope; [21] because the creation itself also will be delivered from the bondage of corruption into the glorious liberty of the children of God. [22] For we know that the whole creation groans and labors with birth pangs together until now. [23] Not only that, but we also who have the firstfruits of the Spirit, even we ourselves groan within ourselves, eagerly waiting for the adoption, the redemption of our body. [24] For we were saved in this hope, but hope that is seen is not hope; for why does one still hope for what he sees? [25] But if we hope for what we do not see, we eagerly wait for it with perseverance.

7. As you read the accounts of Paul's life in the book of Acts and in his own letters, you find that he experienced more than his share of suffering for the cause of Christ. What does he say in this passage about how he viewed his present sufferings? What does he say that all "creation itself" is waiting to one day receive from the Lord (see verses 18–22)?

8. When we accept Christ as our Lord and Savior, we are immediately adopted into God's own family. This spiritual adoption will be "complete" when we receive our resurrected bodies. What should this realization produce in us in spite of our current trials (see verses 23–25)?

REVIEWING THE STORY

Peter addresses his letter to a group of believers in Christ who have been scattered across five provinces in the Roman Empire. These believers found themselves virtually alone in their faith and were pressured on all sides to conform to the culture. Peter encourages them to persevere by remembering the hope they had received in Christ. He notes that the trials they are facing are actually serving to refine their character and will bring glory to God. He assures them of their eternal security in heaven—a hope that has been revealed to them by God.

9. What has God the Father provided through Christ (see 1 Peter 1:3)?

10. What is the purpose of the present trials that you face
(see 1 Peter 1:6–7)?

11. Of what did the Old Testament prophets inquire and search
(see 1 Peter 1:10–11)?

12. What things have been revealed to believers that angels desire to know (see 1 Peter 1:12)?

_____

_____

_____

_____

_____

APPLYING THE MESSAGE

13. How do you respond to the idea that you are merely a "pilgrim" in this world?

_____

_____

_____

_____

_____

_____

_____

14. How does your relationship with Christ strengthen you during trying times?

_____

_____

_____

_____

_____

_____

_____

REFLECTING ON THE MEANING

You are likely not enduring the same kind of pressure or suffering that the believers in Peter's day were experiencing. But you certainly have been through some tough days—moments when it seemed there was no hope. Peter's declaration is that you can have hope in *any* situation because your hope is dependent not on the things of this world but on things much greater.

First, *your hope rests on the power of Jesus' resurrection* (see 1 Peter 1:3). No one had greater reason to celebrate this hope than Peter. He had walked with Jesus. He had trusted in Christ. He had eagerly waited for the Lord to usher in His kingdom. But all of that seemed to be for naught when Jesus was arrested and crucified on a Roman cross. When darkness descended on Good Friday, Peter was downcast, discouraged, and filled with fear.

But then word came that Jesus had risen from the grave! Suddenly, Peter's joy was renewed. His hope was reinstated. Even now, as he wrote this letter, that hope remained. His experience assures you that no matter how dark your situation becomes, your ultimate hope is anchored in Jesus Christ and His power over death. Because He lives . . . *you* will live!

Second, *your hope rests on the promise of your reward* (see verse 4). Peter reminds you that Jesus has promised you an inheritance in heaven. This inheritance—your treasure—is incorruptible. It will never deteriorate or lose value. It will never be taken from you. It has been reserved for you by God, so it cannot be lost.

As a believer, you can be assured of this inheritance because you have already received your first payment. When you were saved, God gave you the Holy Spirit—"the guarantee of our inheritance" (Ephesians 1:14). The Holy Spirit is your ultimate guarantee that one day you will get the rest of the reward that God has promised to you.

Because your hope is built on Jesus' resurrection and the promise of an eternal reward, you are able to praise and rejoice in the midst of your trials. As Peter writes, "In this you greatly rejoice, though now for a little while, if need be, you have been grieved by various trials" (verse 6). Even when everything seems hopeless, you can find hope in your security in Christ.

JOURNALING YOUR RESPONSE

How does the assurance of your salvation and the promise of an eternal reward give you hope?

PURSUING HOLINESS

1 Peter 1:13–25

GETTING STARTED

How would you describe what it means to pursue a life of holiness?

_____

_____

_____

_____

_____

_____

_____

_____

_____

_____

_____

_____

_____

_____

_____

_____

_____

_____

SETTING THE STAGE

As we discussed in the previous lesson, the recipients of Peter's letter were believers who had been scattered throughout several provinces of the Roman Empire. They had settled alongside those who practiced the pagan religions of the day and were being pressured to conform to the norms of society. In that day, religion and society were intertwined, so refusing to participate in a festival or ceremony because of your newfound faith made you stand out in the crowd.

In response to this pressure, Peter challenges them to endure in their faith and continue to cultivate a life of holiness. Now, the word *holiness* usually conjures up images of someone who is culturally out of touch with the times. But its original meaning was to be "set apart" or to "uniquely belong" to someone. For example, in the Old Testament, the vessels of the tabernacle were *holy*. They were set apart and belonged uniquely to God.

In the same way, believers in Christ are called to be uniquely set apart for God . . . to be holy. We are not just to practice *morality,* which is an outward expression of conforming to certain a set of standards. Rather, we are to recognize that God has made us *holy* on the inside. It is possible to be moral and unholy but not holy and immoral. There are many who are moral simply because they fear the consequences of being immoral. But inside, they are unholy.

Morality is what impresses those around us. Holiness is what impresses God. As Peter relates, it represents what we are in the very core of our life as we respond to God. It represents the cleanness of our soul . . . not just the cleanness of our conduct.

EXPLORING THE TEXT

Living Before God Our Father (1 Peter 1:13–21)

> ¹³ Therefore gird up the loins of your mind, be sober, and rest your hope fully upon the grace that is to be brought to you at the revelation

of Jesus Christ; [14] as obedient children, not conforming yourselves to the former lusts, as in your ignorance; [15] but as He who called you is holy, you also be holy in all your conduct, [16] because it is written, "Be holy, for I am holy."

[17] And if you call on the Father, who without partiality judges according to each one's work, conduct yourselves throughout the time of your stay here in fear; [18] knowing that you were not redeemed with corruptible things, like silver or gold, from your aimless conduct received by tradition from your fathers, [19] but with the precious blood of Christ, as of a lamb without blemish and without spot. [20] He indeed was foreordained before the foundation of the world, but was manifest in these last times for you [21] who through Him believe in God, who raised Him from the dead and gave Him glory, so that your faith and hope are in God.

---

1. Peter opened his letter by discussing how his readers could maintain their faith and hope in Christ even in the midst of trials. He now turns his focus on what it *means* to live a holy life before God. What does he say are the traits of the lifestyle of the world? What does Peter call the believers to do instead of conforming to the world (see verses 13–16)?

2. Peter reminds his readers that God will judge their works, so they need to live according to the standard of holiness that he has set for them. How does Peter say they were redeemed? What price did God the Father pay for their salvation (see verses 17–21)?

_____

_____

_____

_____

_____

_____

_____

_____

_____

_____

The Enduring Word (1 Peter 1:22–25)

²² Since you have purified your souls in obeying the truth through the Spirit in sincere love of the brethren, love one another fervently with a pure heart, ²³ having been born again, not of corruptible seed but incorruptible, through the word of God which lives and abides forever, ²⁴ because

"All flesh is as grass,
And all the glory of man as the flower of the grass.
The grass withers,
And its flower falls away,
²⁵ But the word of the LORD endures forever."

Now this is the word which by the gospel was preached to you.

3. Peter acknowledges that his recipients have been seeking to "purify their souls" and lead holy lives before God. What are two ways they have done this? What does Peter remind them about the nature of the truth they have received (see verses 22–23)?

_____

_____

_____

_____

_____

_____

4. Peter quotes from Isaiah 40:6–8 to show that everything in this world will pass away but God's word will always endure. When Isaiah gave this prophecy, the people of Israel were living in exile and facing hostility and pressure to conform to the culture around them. How would this prophecy have given Peter's readers hope in their situation (verses 23–25)?

_____

_____

_____

_____

_____

GOING DEEPER

The idea that God's people should lead holy lives is a theme that runs throughout the New Testament . . . and the entire Bible. As Peter noted, God has always commanded His people, "Be holy, for I am holy" (1 Peter 1:16; Leviticus 11:44). The apostle Paul also pointed out the need for believers to continually seek to lead holy lives. In his letter to the church

17

in Rome, he asks his readers to move from being "slaves of sin" to "slaves of God." In his first letter to the Thessalonians, he issues more specific instructions for how to maintain purity and holiness.

From Slaves of Sin to Slaves of God (Romans 6:15–18)

[15] What then? Shall we sin because we are not under law but under grace? Certainly not! [16] Do you not know that to whom you present yourselves slaves to obey, you are that one's slaves whom you obey, whether of sin leading to death, or of obedience leading to righteousness? [17] But God be thanked that though you were slaves of sin, yet you obeyed from the heart that form of doctrine to which you were delivered. [18] And having been set free from sin, you became slaves of righteousness.

5. In the preceding verses, Paul stated that a life of habitual sin is incompatible with the pursuit of holiness. In this passage, he addresses the issue of "occasional" types of sin that seem harmless in the moment. What truth is essential to remember when believers are tempted to downplay such "misdemeanor" offenses (see verses 15–17)?

6. Paul uses the past tense when referring to his readers' slavery to sin. For what does he thank God as it relates to their current state? What are they now (see verses 17–18)?

_____

_____

_____

_____

_____

_____

_____

_____

_____

_____

_____

_____

A Plea for Purity (1 Thessalonians 4:1–8)

[1] Finally then, brethren, we urge and exhort in the Lord Jesus that you should abound more and more, just as you received from us how you ought to walk and to please God; [2] for you know what commandments we gave you through the Lord Jesus.

[3] For this is the will of God, your sanctification: that you should abstain from sexual immorality; [4] that each of you should know how to possess his own vessel in sanctification and honor, [5] not in passion of lust, like the Gentiles who do not know God; [6] that no one should take advantage of and defraud his brother in this matter, because the Lord is the avenger of all such, as we also forewarned you and testified. [7] For God did not call us to uncleanness, but in holiness. [8] Therefore he who rejects this does not reject man, but God, who has also given us His Holy Spirit.

7. Paul's instruction to "abound more and more" means the pursuit of holiness is not finished until we get to heaven. What should be our focus as we pursue holiness (see verses 1–2)?

_____

_____

_____

_____

8. The commands that Paul issued to the believers in Thessalonica would have put them out of step with their culture, which viewed sexual immorality either indifferently or favorably. Regardless, what does he say is *God's* standard for holiness? What warning does he gives for those who choose to disregard this advice (see verses 3–8)?

_____

_____

_____

_____

REVIEWING THE STORY

The early Christians were scattered in communities throughout the Roman Empire. As a result, they were frequently pressured by the pagan societies in which they lived to adapt to the lifestyle of the culture. Peter recognizes this pressure on them to conform to their "former lusts" (1:14), so he reiterates the fact that they have been "set apart" by God and refined by Him to live in a different manner. He urges them to obey the truths of God they have learned, continue to love one another, and pursue God's will in everything they do.

9. What does holy conduct look like (see 1 Peter 1:13–14)?

_____

_____

_____

_____

_____

_____

_____

10. Of what can we be confident as we pursue holiness (see 1 Peter 1:17–21)?

_____

_____

_____

_____

_____

_____

11. How does holiness affect the way we interact with other believers (see 1 Peter 1:22–23)?

_____

_____

_____

_____

_____

_____

_____

12. Why should we base our conduct on the Word of God (see 1 Peter 1:24–25)?

_____

_____

_____

_____

_____

_____

APPLYING THE MESSAGE

13. What are some of the pressures that you have faced to conform to the ways of the world?

_____

_____

_____

_____

_____

_____

14. How does it help you to endure in your pursuit of holiness when you consider what it cost God to send His Son into this world to redeem you of sin?

_____

_____

_____

_____

_____

_____

REFLECTING ON THE MEANING

The apostle Peter opens this section of his letter with a command for all believers. As he writes, "Gird up the loins of your mind, be sober, and rest your hope fully upon the grace that is to be brought to you at the revelation of Jesus Christ" (1 Peter 1:13). As you look at Peter's statement, three key strategies emerge on how to cultivate holiness in your life.

First, you are to "gird up the loins" of your mind. The phrase "gird up the loins" was a figure of speech in Peter's day that referred to the act of tucking a flowing robe into a belt in order to move around with greater speed and efficiency. It conveys the idea of readiness, discipline, and being prepared for action. Applying this metaphor to your mind means to focus on a particular goal. It infers cutting out "sloppy thinking," especially when it comes to God's Word. You must be willing to embrace God's Word on its own terms, instead of trying to filter it through any cultural preferences. You cannot lose your edge in holiness.

Second, you are to "be sober." The term *sober,* in this context, refers to moral alertness and maintaining control of your speech and conduct. It describes a life of discipline and responsibility. Those who are Spirit-filled are not carried away into extravagance of behavior but act like people who are in full possession of themselves. Obviously, this was in stark contrast to the society of the day, which was frequently given to excess.

Third, you are to "rest your hope fully" on the expectation of Christ's return. The hope that believers in Christ possess is rooted not in this world but on the eternal promises of God that will be realized when Jesus returns to this earth. It is because of this living hope within you that are able to endure and persevere in leading a godly life . . . even though you may be ostracized or penalized by society as a result. In the meantime, you lean on God's grace.

Peter's message is that if you want to survive in a hostile world, you have to remember that it is temporary. You have an inheritance in heaven that has been reserved just for you. One day, at the revelation of Jesus Christ, you will understand how all the trials you have endured have served a purpose. In the meantime, you can avoid being absorbed into the wickedness of the world by keeping your eyes fixed on the future. Someday, all that God has promised will be yours. Contemplating that truth is what keep will keep you going.

JOURNALING YOUR RESPONSE

What are some ways that you can implement these strategies to live in greater holiness?

_____

_____

_____

_____

_____

_____

_____

_____

_____

_____

_____

_____

_____

_____

_____

_____

_____

_____

_____

_____

_____

_____

_____

PURSUING SPIRITUAL GROWTH

1 Peter 2:1–12

GETTING STARTED

What evidence of spiritual growth do you see in your life?

SETTING THE STAGE

Peter knew the enemy's strategies against believers in Christ only too well. On the night that Jesus was arrested in the Garden of Gethesemane, Satan convinced him and the other disciples that they had placed their hopes in a false Messiah, and all "forsook Him and fled" (Matthew 26:56). When Peter later went to the courtyard where Jesus was being tried, he caved into the pressure—and fear—of those around him who accused him of being a follower of Christ. Peter denied knowing Him three times.

Now, writing to believers in the churches many years later, Peter could see the strategies that Satan was employing to discourage them and impede their effectiveness in sharing the gospel. As we discussed previously, the first strategy was to take away their hope—to keep them from believing there was something greater beyond this world. A second strategy was to try to get them to meld into the culture from which they were trying to stand apart.

However, Peter recognized that the enemy was also employing a third strategy. Satan was attempting to get the believers to simply maintain their "spiritual status quo." The devil wanted them to be content with where they were in their relationship with God, take away any sense of the need for progress, and ultimately hamper them from growing spiritually. Peter combats this strategy by stressing the need for them to always continue *growing* in their faith. In the Christian life, there is no such thing as status quo. We are either growing and moving forward in our Christian experience . . . or we are stagnating and moving in the wrong direction.

In this next section, Peter makes the natural transition from maintaining our hope in Christ and pursuing God's standards of holiness to growing in our faith. Using one of the most memorable analogies in the New Testament—that of newborn babes—he emphasizes the importance of nourishing ourselves on God's Word. It is only in this manner that we will continue to mature in our spiritual life.

Exploring the Text

Our Inheritance in Christ (1 Peter 2:1–8)

---

[1] Therefore, laying aside all malice, all deceit, hypocrisy, envy, and all evil speaking, [2] as newborn babes, desire the pure milk of the word, that you may grow thereby, [3] if indeed you have tasted that the Lord is gracious.

[4] Coming to Him as to a living stone, rejected indeed by men, but chosen by God and precious, [5] you also, as living stones, are being built up a spiritual house, a holy priesthood, to offer up spiritual sacrifices acceptable to God through Jesus Christ. [6] Therefore it is also contained in the Scripture,

> "Behold, I lay in Zion
> A chief cornerstone, elect, precious,
> And he who believes on Him will by no means be put to shame."

[7] Therefore, to you who believe, He is precious; but to those who are disobedient,

> "The stone which the builders rejected
> Has become the chief cornerstone,"

[8] and

> "A stone of stumbling
> And a rock of offense."

They stumble, being disobedient to the word, to which they also were appointed.

---

1. Peter begins this section with the word *therefore*, which indicates he is bringing all he discussed previously to a main point. The sum of the imperatives he has just mentioned regarding holiness and love must lead to spiritual transformation. How does the analogy of the newborn babe represent what he wants them to pursue (see verses 1–3)?

_____

_____

_____

_____

_____

_____

_____

_____

2. Peter notes that spiritual growth is vital not just for the individual but also for the church as a whole. His readers are "living stones" that God is using to build into a "spiritual house." Peter goes on to cite several references from the Old Testament to support his point (see Psalm 118:22, Isaiah 28:16, and Isaiah 8:14). How does Peter use these passages to describe the believers? How does he characterize those who reject Christ (see 1 Peter 2:4–8)?

_____

_____

_____

_____

_____

_____

_____

_____

_____

Living Before the World (1 Peter 2:9–12)

⁹ But you are a chosen generation, a royal priesthood, a holy nation, His own special people, that you may proclaim the praises of Him who called you out of darkness into His marvelous light; ¹⁰ who once were not a people but are now the people of God, who had not obtained mercy but now have obtained mercy.

¹¹ Beloved, I beg you as sojourners and pilgrims, abstain from fleshly lusts which war against the soul, ¹² having your conduct honorable among the Gentiles, that when they speak against you as evildoers, they may, by your good works which they observe, glorify God in the day of visitation.

3. Peter emphasizes his point by employing a number of Old Testament metaphors that describe how God viewed the Israelite people (see Exodus 19:5–6, Deuteronomy 7:6, 1 Samuel 12:22, and Isaiah 62:2). The believers have been given this same status in God's eyes as a result of their faith in Christ. What responsibility does Peter say comes with that privilege (see verses 9–10)?

_____

_____

_____

_____

_____

_____

_____

4. As noted previously, Peter holds that followers of Christ are "sojourners and pilgrims" on this earth and that their true citizenship is in heaven. As a result of this status, what are believers able to resist in this world? What impact does their honorable conduct and progression in spiritual growth have on others (see verses 11–12)?

_____

_____

_____

_____

GOING DEEPER

Several other New Testament authors also write on the need for believers in Christ to be continually striving to grow in spiritual maturity. In the apostle Paul's letter to the Ephesians, he offers a vivid description of what it looks like when believers are growing in their faith and using their God-given gifts to support the work of the church. The author of Hebrews, employing a different tact, issues a stark warning about the perils of not growing in one's faith.

Growing in Spiritual Gifts (Ephesians 4:11–16)

11 And He Himself gave some to be apostles, some prophets, some evangelists, and some pastors and teachers, 12 for the equipping of the saints for the work of ministry, for the edifying of the body of Christ, 13 till we all come to the unity of the faith and of the knowledge of the Son of God, to a perfect man, to the measure of the stature of the fullness of Christ; 14 that we should no longer be children, tossed to and fro and carried about with every wind of doctrine, by the trickery of men, in the cunning craftiness of deceitful plotting, 15 but, speaking the truth in love, may grow up in all things into Him who is the head—Christ— 16 from whom the whole body, joined and knit together by what every joint supplies, according to the effective working by which every part does its share, causes growth of the body for the edifying of itself in love.

5. Paul's statement, "the measure of the stature of the fullness of Christ" (verse 13), refers to our growth in Christ. What are some of the gifts we may receive if we are growing in our faith? How are we to use those gifts in the body of Christ (see verses 11–13)?

_____

_____

_____

_____

_____

_____

6. Spiritual "children"—believers who don't grow in their faith—are liabilities in the church. How does Paul describe these types of individuals and the dangers they face? What does he urge followers of Jesus to do instead (see verses 14–16)?

_____

_____

_____

_____

_____

_____

The Peril of Not Progressing (Hebrews 6:1–8)

[1] Therefore, leaving the discussion of the elementary principles of Christ, let us go on to perfection, not laying again the foundation of repentance from dead works and of faith toward God, [2] of the doctrine of baptisms, of laying on of hands, of resurrection of the dead, and of eternal judgment. [3] And this we will do if God permits.

⁴ For it is impossible for those who were once enlightened, and have tasted the heavenly gift, and have become partakers of the Holy Spirit, ⁵ and have tasted the good word of God and the powers of the age to come, ⁶ if they fall away, to renew them again to repentance, since they crucify again for themselves the Son of God, and put Him to an open shame.

⁷ For the earth which drinks in the rain that often comes upon it, and bears herbs useful for those by whom it is cultivated, receives blessing from God; ⁸ but if it bears thorns and briers, it is rejected and near to being cursed, whose end is to be burned.

---

5. The author's use of the term "elementary principles" refers to the basic building blocks of the Christian faith. These principles are essential for all believers in starting out in their faith . . . but they should never be the ending point. What should the next steps be for followers of Christ after they are grounded in these basic truths (see verses 1–3)?

6. The writer describes the consequences of "tasting" the Word of God, experiencing its impact, and then falling away—or failing to grow. What are these dire consequences? What analogy does the author use to then drive his point home (see verses 4–8)?

REVIEWING THE STORY

Peter emphasizes the Christian life is one of constant growth. Just like "newborn babes," we are to desire the "milk of the word" and grow in spiritual maturity. This process of growth benefits not only ourselves but also the community of believers to which we belong. As followers of Christ, we are "living stones," rejected by the world, that God is using to build into a "spiritual house" to bless others and bring them to Him. We need to continue to treat God's truth and wisdom as precious so we will grow in our faith and not be like those disobedient to God.

9. What must we lay aside in order to grow spiritually (see 1 Peter 2:1)?

_____

_____

_____

_____

10. If we have tasted that the Lord is gracious, what should our desire be (see 1 Peter 2:2–3)?

_____

_____

_____

_____

11. What is our responsibility as part of the royal priesthood (see 1 Peter 2:9–10)?

_____

_____

_____

_____

12. What happens when we conduct ourselves honorably
(see 1 Peter 2:11–12)?

_____

_____

_____

_____

_____

_____

APPLYING THE MESSAGE

13. What are some ways that you are seeking to grow in your
relationship with God?

_____

_____

_____

_____

_____

_____

_____

14. How have you been able to help others recently to grow in
their faith?

_____

_____

_____

_____

_____

_____

_____

REFLECTING ON THE MEANING

The Christian life is like riding a bicycle. As long as you are pushing the pedals, watching where you are going, and correcting your course, you will move forward and reach your destination. But if you just sit there, it is likely you will fall off . . . and you certainly won't make progress. In the Christian life, just as in riding a bicycle, there is no standing still. Peter understood this truth, and in this section of his letter, he identifies three steps for maintaining spiritual growth.

The first step is renunciation. Peter writes, "Therefore, [lay] aside all malice, all deceit, hypocrisy, envy, and all evil speaking" (2:1). Before you can grow, you must do away with anything that will hinder your growth. You renounce any intent to do evil to others, any trickery to hurt others, and any hypocrisy, envy, or evil words used against others. These sins will destroy your appetite for God's Word, which is the source of your nourishment and growth. A spiritually healthy Christian is a hungry Christian! The more completely you renounce evil thoughts, attitudes, and actions, the more your appetite for God's Word will grow.

The second step is aspiration. Peter states, "As newborn babes, desire the pure milk of the word" (verse 2). Just as milk is the perfect food for a baby, so God's Word is the perfect food for believers. You should aspire to read it, study it, and let its truth nourish your soul. You need to maintain your hunger and desire for its nourishment. You must allow its truth to take root in your life by asking pertinent questions and looking for ways to apply it.

The third step is occupation. Peter describes believers in Christ as "a holy priesthood [who] offer up spiritual sacrifices acceptable to God through Jesus Christ" (verse 5). This is your occupation . . . the work you are called to pursue. As a "priest," you offer your body to God as sacrifice to do His work. You ask Him to lead your life so you can accomplish His will. You offer your money as a sacrifice to spread the gospel, your praise and singing to God, and the sacrifice of your good works by sharing your resources and conducting yourself as a loving and gracious person. These sacrifices represent the natural outward result of your internal spiritual growth.

JOURNALING YOUR RESPONSE

Which of these three steps are the most challenging for you? Why?

SUBMITTING TO AUTHORITY

1 Peter 2:13–25

GETTING STARTED

How do you decide whether to follow a workplace (or government) mandate?

_____

_____

_____

_____

_____

_____

_____

_____

_____

_____

_____

_____

SETTING THE STAGE

Peter has emphasized that we must persevere in our faith, lead holy lives, and grow in our relationship with God. However, it is not enough for us to merely adopt these godly traits and live in isolation. God has called us to be citizens of the world. This means we are to influence the world for Him even as we respect the authorities that He has put in place.

This next section of Peter's letter is thus a godsend for those who are uncertain about their role in society—especially in the workplace. After all, each of us face situations each day on the job that test our patience, endurance, and spiritual resolve. The boss hands us a list of correspondence at the end of the day that has to be completed immediately—work that could have done earlier if he or she had been more considerate. A teammate constantly presents our ideas as her own. Another coworker builds up his ego by putting us down.

It is not always easy to know how we, as believers in Christ, should respond in these situations. How are we to function in adverse circumstances? How should we respond when others are unfair and provoke us to anger? According to Peter, the key is *submission*—a word that is provocative in its own right. We naturally resist the idea of submitting to others because it feels like weakness. Submission means giving territory that belongs to us . . . and we have been conditioned to always protect our territory. We simply do not *want* to yield to another.

Yet it is this spirit of submission that Peter urges us to pursue. He implores followers of Jesus to submit to the powers that have been placed over us—*even if those powers are ungodly*. In this next section of his letter, he shows us how to navigate this often-tricky road.

EXPLORING THE TEXT

Submission to Government (1 Peter 2:13–17)

¹³ Therefore submit yourselves to every ordinance of man for the Lord's sake, whether to the king as supreme, ¹⁴ or to governors, as to those who are sent by him for the punishment of evildoers and for the praise of those who do good. ¹⁵ For this is the will of God, that by doing good you may put to silence the ignorance of foolish

men— ¹⁶ as free, yet not using liberty as a cloak for vice, but as bondservants of God. ¹⁷ Honor all people. Love the brotherhood. Fear God. Honor the king.

---

1. Peter recognized that being a good witness for Christ in the world required believers to first be good citizens of the world. This meant following the established rules in a society—a difficult proposition for first-century Jews who recognized no authority but God. How extensive does Peter say the believers' submission to authority must be (see verses 13–14)?

_____

_____

_____

_____

_____

_____

2. Throughout Peter's letter, he emphasizes the importance of good Christian conduct. What is the end result Peter sees of believers "doing good"? What impact will their submission to the government authorities have on all who witness it (see verses 15–17)?

_____

_____

_____

_____

_____

_____

_____

Submission to Masters (1 Peter 2:18–25)

[18] Servants, be submissive to your masters with all fear, not only to the good and gentle, but also to the harsh. [19] For this is commendable, if because of conscience toward God one endures grief, suffering wrongfully. [20] For what credit is it if, when you are beaten for your faults, you take it patiently? But when you do good and suffer, if you take it patiently, this is commendable before God. [21] For to this you were called, because Christ also suffered for us, leaving us an example, that you should follow His steps:

[22] "Who committed no sin,
Nor was deceit found in His mouth";

[23] who, when He was reviled, did not revile in return; when He suffered, He did not threaten, but committed Himself to Him who judges righteously; [24] who Himself bore our sins in His own body on the tree, that we, having died to sins, might live for righteousness—by whose stripes you were healed. [25] For you were like sheep going astray, but have now returned to the Shepherd and Overseer of your souls.

3. For Peter, submission to those in authority does not end with government officials. He sees the need for submission in other realms of society—even in the servant-master relationships of his day. What does Peter advise that servants do when relating to their masters? What benefit does he envision even if this results in suffering (see verses 18–20)?

_____

_____

_____

_____

_____

_____

4. Peter understands his instruction to submit to human authorities will be difficult for his readers to accept. What does he call them to remember in this regard when it comes to the suffering that Jesus endured for their sake? How should Jesus' example motivate them to submit to even the harsh authorities that were placed over them (see verses 21–25)?

_____

_____

_____

_____

_____

_____

_____

_____

_____

_____

GOING DEEPER

In the book of Acts, Peter states that people "ought to obey God rather than men" (5:29) when those in authority are commanding us to do something that goes against God's laws. Otherwise, we are to obey those leaders whom God has put over us. The apostle Paul, in his letter to the Romans, likewise saw the need to advise believers in Christ to submit to the authorities that God had placed in the world. The author of Hebrews also drew a connection between the sacrifices that believers offer to God and their willingness to submit human authorities.

God's Ministers in the World (Romans 13:1–7)

> ¹ Let every soul be subject to the governing authorities. For there is no authority except from God, and the authorities that exist are appointed by God. ² Therefore whoever resists the authority resists

the ordinance of God, and those who resist will bring judgment on themselves. [3] For rulers are not a terror to good works, but to evil. Do you want to be unafraid of the authority? Do what is good, and you will have praise from the same. [4] For he is God's minister to you for good. But if you do evil, be afraid; for he does not bear the sword in vain; for he is God's minister, an avenger to execute wrath on him who practices evil. [5] Therefore you must be subject, not only because of wrath but also for conscience' sake. [6] For because of this you also pay taxes, for they are God's ministers attending continually to this very thing. [7] Render therefore to all their due: taxes to whom taxes are due, customs to whom customs, fear to whom fear, honor to whom honor.

---

5. As noted previously, the zealous Jews of Paul's day held there is no authority but God . . . so they were not required to submit to any human authority. Paul does not deny that God has *ultimate* authority, but what does he say about how human authorities gained their position? What is the person who resists human authority actually doing (see verses 1–2)?

_____

_____

_____

_____

_____

_____

_____

_____

_____

6. Paul notes that human authorities serve a function in the world— they punish wrongdoers and keep the peace. In this regard, they can be seen as God's ministers. Given this, what must Christians do to support them in their work (see verses 3–7)?

_____

_____

_____

_____

_____

_____

Obeying Rulers (Hebrews 13:15–17)

[15] Therefore by Him let us continually offer the sacrifice of praise to God, that is, the fruit of our lips, giving thanks to His name. [16] But do not forget to do good and to share, for with such sacrifices God is well pleased. [17] Obey those who rule over you, and be submissive, for they watch out for your souls, as those who must give account. Let them do so with joy and not with grief, for that would be unprofitable for you.

7. The author of Hebrews notes that believers can "offer the sacrifice of praise" to God through the words they say. What does it mean to _continually_ offer these types of sacrifices? What else does the author call on believers to do (see verses 15–16)?

_____

_____

_____

_____

_____

_____

8. Submitting to human authorities represents another form of sacrifice in a believer's life. What does the writer of this letter say about the role of these authorities? What responsibilities do they bear in their governance? (see verses 16–17)?

REVIEWING THE STORY

Peter instructs believers to submit to "every ordinance of man," which includes both governing authorities and, if they are servants, their masters. As they do this, they will serve as an example to others of what it means to follow Christ and thus "silence the ignorance of foolish men." Even if their obedience leads to suffering, they are to look to the example of Jesus, their Lord, who also wrongfully suffered when he died for their sins on the cross.

9. What is God's will as it relates to submitting to government (see 1 Peter 2:13–14)?

10. How does Peter say believers should act in society
(see 1 Peter 2:17)?

_____

_____

_____

_____

_____

_____

_____

11. What happens when believers remain patient even in suffering
(see 1 Peter 2: 20)?

_____

_____

_____

_____

_____

_____

_____

12. How did Jesus respond when He was reviled by others
(see 1 Peter 2:23–24)?

_____

_____

_____

_____

_____

_____

APPLYING THE MESSAGE

13. Under what conditions is it the most difficult for you to submit to authority?

_____

_____

_____

_____

_____

_____

_____

14. How do you typically respond when you feel that something in authority (such as a boss at work) is treating you unfairly or causing you to suffer?

_____

_____

_____

_____

_____

_____

_____

REFLECTING ON THE MEANING

In this section of Peter's letter, he points out that the best way for believers in Christ to learn to submit to authority is to look at Jesus' example. The Bible says that Jesus suffered without any reason. He never said or did anything wrong. No one else can make such a claim! We are typically responsible, to some degree, for the problems we face. But Jesus was not. As we look at His example, we uncover three ways that He submitted even to unjust authorities.

First, Jesus submitted without response. Peter writes, "When He was reviled, [He] did not revile in return" (1 Peter 2:23). The word *revile* means to insult another person with abusive speech. Christ was frequently reviled by the Jewish religious leaders of the day. He was reviled by those who did not believe that He was the Messiah. He was reviled by those who cruelly mocked Him on the way to the cross. Jesus clearly had the power and authority to fight back (see Matthew 26:53). Yet Jesus chose to submit to the will of God and be led to the cross.

Second, Jesus submitted without retaliation. Peter writes, "When He suffered, He did not threaten" (verse 23). It is human nature to want to pay others back in kind when we feel that we have been wronged. We want to retaliate and get even—to make them feel just a bit of the pain that we experienced. At the least, we want to hold a grudge! But Jesus refused to retaliate against those who were unjustly wronging Him. Even as He suffered on the cross, He asked God to forgive them for their deeds, "for they do not know what they do" (Luke 23:34).

Third, Jesus suffered without reservation. Peter writes, "[He] committed Himself to Him who judges righteously" (1 Peter 2:23). The word *commit,* in this context, means to deliver oneself into the hands of another. Judas *delivered* Jesus up to the Roman soldiers. Pilate *delivered* Jesus up to those who wanted to crucify Him. Jesus, in turn, delivered Himself up to God. As we read in the Gospels, on the cross, He cried out, "Father, into Your hands I commit My spirit" (Luke 23:46).

Following Jesus' example in submission will not come naturally to us. We will not get it right the first time. We will be tempted to give up along the way. But if we were able to follow Jesus' lead, it would revolutionize our culture. People everywhere would be talking about our faith in Christ that is so unusual and dynamic. Everyone in our world and sphere of influence would notice . . . and our lives would point them to the grace and mercy of God.

JOURNALING YOUR RESPONSE

How could you follow Jesus' example the next time you are tempted to rebel against those in authority over you?

SUBMITTING IN THE HOME

1 Peter 3:1–12

GETTING STARTED

What does submission look like in relationships within your family?

_____

_____

_____

_____

_____

_____

_____

_____

_____

_____

_____

_____

_____

_____

_____

_____

_____

_____

SETTING THE STAGE

The key word that runs throughout this chapter of Peter's letter is *submission*. The apostle has discussed the responsibilities that Christians have in submitting to their government. He has spoken to those believers who were slaves and advised them what they needed to do to submit to their masters. Obviously, the application to us today is in the workplace, where we have to learn how to submit to our employer and show respect to our fellow workers.

Peter now turns the conversation on submission to matters of the home. Unfortunately, his words in this section are often misunderstood today . . . and generally viewed by society as controversial. Critics say that it disempowers women and represents an outmoded patriarchal system. However, there is no section at the end of the Bible for amendments. Neither is there an à la carte menu that allows us to choose just those commands that look good to us.

So, in this lesson, we will wrestle with Peter's marital instructions. But in order to do so effectively, we fist need to understand the context in which the letter was written. In the Roman Empire, women occupied a low position in society. When many of those women came to Christ, they felt as if they had been given real value for the first time in their lives. This sudden awareness caused them to rethink their relationships with their husbands.

Many of the women were married to men who cared nothing for the Christ they had come to know. Some thus concluded their new allegiance to Christ meant they no longer had any responsibilities to their husband and marriages. Their reactions were similar to those who came to Christ and assumed their new citizenship in heaven canceled any responsibilities of their citizenship on earth. Or those slaves who came to Christ and thought that because they were now Christians, they no longer had to be subservient to their masters.

In all cases, these believers appealed to a higher authority. Peter did not contradict this idea that they needed to submit to God's authority *first* in their lives. However, he wanted them to understand that God had established certain patterns of human authority in all of these relationships that He expected them to follow. Those patterns involved *submission*.

EXPLORING THE TEXT

Submission to Husbands (1 Peter 3:1–6)

¹ Wives, likewise, be submissive to your own husbands, that even if some do not obey the word, they, without a word, may be won by the conduct of their wives, ² when they observe your chaste conduct accompanied by fear. ³ Do not let your adornment be merely outward—arranging the hair, wearing gold, or putting on fine apparel— ⁴ rather let it be the hidden person of the heart, with the incorruptible beauty of a gentle and quiet spirit, which is very precious in the sight of God. ⁵ For in this manner, in former times, the holy women who trusted in God also adorned themselves, being submissive to their own husbands, ⁶ as Sarah obeyed Abraham, calling him lord, whose daughters you are if you do good and are not afraid with any terror.

1. Peter's use of the word *likewise* indicates he is continuing his general discussion on the need for believers to submit to authority in all phases of life. This applies in marriages . . . even if the spouse is not a believer. What does Peter say non-believing husbands will come to understand Christianity through the example of their wives (see verses 1–2)?

_____

_____

_____

_____

_____

_____

_____

2. Peter's discussion on outward "adornments" is not meant to prohibit wives for wearing jewelry or having nice clothes but to remind them to focus more on their internal character. The pagans of the day viewed virtue as praiseworthy, so such traits reflected well on Christ. How does the example that Peter uses help to reinforce his point (see verses 3–6)?

_____

_____

_____

_____

_____

Called to Blessing (1 Peter 3:8–12)

⁷ Husbands, likewise, dwell with them with understanding, giving honor to the wife, as to the weaker vessel, and as being heirs together of the grace of life, that your prayers may not be hindered.

⁸ Finally, all of you be of one mind, having compassion for one another; love as brothers, be tenderhearted, be courteous; ⁹ not returning evil for evil or reviling for reviling, but on the contrary blessing, knowing that you were called to this, that you may inherit a blessing. ¹⁰ For

"He who would love life
And see good days,
Let him refrain his tongue from evil,
And his lips from speaking deceit.
¹¹ Let him turn away from evil and do good;
Let him seek peace and pursue it.
¹² For the eyes of the LORD are on the righteous,
And His ears are open to their prayers;
But the face of the LORD is against those who do evil."

3. Peter's instructions for believers to submit also applies to husbands. What four instructions does he give? What happens when a husband treats his wife with honor (see verse 7)?

_____

_____

_____

_____

_____

_____

_____

4. Peter closes with a general instruction for all believers to be "of one mind," which in this case refers to having the mind of Christ. What happens when believers share such a mindset? What does the passage that Peter quotes from Psalm 34:12–16 reveal about the blessing they will receive when they love and respect one another (see verses 8–12)?

_____

_____

_____

_____

_____

_____

_____

GOING DEEPER

In Paul's letter to the Ephesians, he offers similar instructions to Christian households in regard to how husbands and wives are to treat one another and function in their marriage in obedience to the Lord. Jesus also spoke of marriage in response to a question from the Pharisees (a strict religious group in Israel) on God's expectations for couples in a marriage.

Marriage, Christ, and the Church (Ephesians 5:22–28)

²² Wives, submit to your own husbands, as to the Lord. ²³ For the husband is head of the wife, as also Christ is head of the church; and He is the Savior of the body. ²⁴ Therefore, just as the church is subject to Christ, so let the wives be to their own husbands in everything.

²⁵ Husbands, love your wives, just as Christ also loved the church and gave Himself for her, ²⁶ that He might sanctify and cleanse her with the washing of water by the word, ²⁷ that He might present her to Himself a glorious church, not having spot or wrinkle or any such thing, but that she should be holy and without blemish. ²⁸ So husbands ought to love their own wives as their own bodies; he who loves his wife loves himself.

5. The Greek word for *submit* that Paul employs in this passage was a military term in his day. It referred to the act of a soldier voluntarily putting himself in rank under another person. In submitting to their husbands, to whom are wives also submitting (see verses 22–24)?

----

6. Paul stresses that husbands also have responsibilities in the relationship. What are his instructions? How does he expand on the example of Christ (see verses 25–28)?

God's Plan for Marriage (Matthew 19:3–9)

³ The Pharisees also came to Him, testing Him, and saying to Him, "Is it lawful for a man to divorce his wife for just any reason?"

⁴ And He answered and said to them, "Have you not read that He who made them at the beginning 'made them male and female,' ⁵ and said, 'For this reason a man shall leave his father and mother and be joined to his wife, and the two shall become one flesh'? ⁶ So then, they are no longer two but one flesh. Therefore what God has joined together, let not man separate."

⁷ They said to Him, "Why then did Moses command to give a certificate of divorce, and to put her away?"

⁸ He said to them, "Moses, because of the hardness of your hearts, permitted you to divorce your wives, but from the beginning it was not so. ⁹ And I say to you, whoever divorces his wife, except for sexual immorality, and marries another, commits adultery; and whoever marries her who is divorced commits adultery."

7. How does Jesus respond to the question from the Pharisees about whether it is lawful for a man to divorce his wife for any reason (see verses 3–6)?

8. What reason does Jesus provide for why divorce was allowed in the Old Testament? What does this say about God's plan for marriage (see verses 7–9)?

_____

_____

_____

_____

_____

REVIEWING THE STORY

Peter addresses Christian wives in the church who had gained a sense of respect and importance in their faith that they did not get from their husbands or Roman society. Some of these women assumed their Christian freedom gave them the right to change the dynamics of their marital relationship. Peter addresses their misconceptions by showing how their submission reflects well on Christ and can actually lead to their husbands accepting the message of the gospel. He then issues instructions to husbands about the importance of showing understanding, honor, and genuine love to their wives.

9. What does Peter say about actions speaking louder than words (see 1 Peter 3:1)?

_____

_____

_____

_____

_____

10. Why does a husband need to show his wife honor and understanding (see 1 Peter 3:7)?

11. What attitudes should be present in believers' interactions (see 1 Peter 3:8–9)?

12. What are the keys to loving life and seeing good days (see 1 Peter 3:10–12)?

APPLYING THE MESSAGE

13. How would you summarize how God expects husbands and wives to treat one another?

_____

_____

_____

_____

_____

_____

14. When is it the most difficult for you to "be of one mind" and have compassion on those people who are closest to you?

_____

_____

_____

_____

_____

_____

_____

_____

REFLECTING ON THE MEANING

Peter directs the bulk of his instructions in this section of his letter to wives in Christian households. He wants them to reject the false idea that was evidently flourishing in the early church that their new allegiance to Christ meant they could turn their backs on their former allegiance to their spouses. But Peter has instructions for Christian husbands as well.

In fact, he offers four distinct challenges in 1 Peter 3:7 for all husbands of the faith to follow.

First, a husband should be sympathetic to his wife's personality. In the first-century Roman world, wives were regarded as a property to be owned rather than a partner to love. Peter says that in Christian households, this idea must be replaced with a genuine respect and thoughtfulness on the husband's part to understand his wife.

Second, a husband should be sensitive to his wife's frailty. Once again, there is controversy in making such a statement, but this is not meant to deny the strength of women. It is simply an acknowledgment of the disparity between the physical strength of a man and a woman. Such disparity calls for a gentle and courteous attitude on the part of the husband to his wife. This leaves no room whatsoever for abusive behavior of any kind.

Third, a husband should be secure in his wife's equality. In every group setting there has to be a leader, and God has ordained the husband to be the head of the home. For this reason, those who are members of the household should submit to the husband's authority. However, *before God,* there is no difference between husband and wife. All are "heirs together of the grace of life." Peter is thus saying to husbands that while a husband has a responsibility as the head of his home and his wife, before God the two of them are not any different. Both are equally responsible, esteemed, and loved. They have equality.

Fourth, a husband should be serious about his wife's spirituality. Peter states that husbands should follow this guidance so their "prayers may not be hindered." This suggests God is so concerned that Christian husbands live in a loving way with their wives that He interrupts His relationship with them when they are not doing so. No husband can have an effective prayer life unless he lives with his wife in a loving and understanding way.

So, we see that Peter's instructions for a wife to be submissive to her husband is held in balance with his command for a husband to treat his wife with love and respect. A husband understands that he is to treat his wife with honor because they are both equals before God. When this happens, it brings God glory and the marriage flourishes.

JOURNALING YOUR RESPONSE

What are some practical ways that you could demonstrate love and respect to a person you care about in your life?

SUFFERING IN THIS WORLD

1 Peter 3:13–22

GETTING STARTED

What are some of the ways you have wrestled with the question of why suffering exists?

_____

_____

_____

_____

_____

_____

_____

_____

_____

_____

SETTING THE STAGE

Humans have always struggled with the reality of suffering and evil in this world. How can they exist in a world that was created by a loving God? It's an age-old question that goes back to as far as there has been belief in God. In the Old Testament, we read how a righteous man named Job endured suffering and exclaimed, "Why did I not die at birth" (Job 3:11). When a particular evil reaches a tipping point, or when suffering hits home in a personal way, the question becomes a desperate plea and causes us to likewise cry out, "why?"

Some people explain the existence of suffering and evil by questioning God's love. The reasoning goes like this. If God is omnipotent (all-powerful), He can do anything, which includes putting an end to suffering and evil. The fact that He chooses not to—that He allows people to suffer and evil to continue—proves that He is not loving. Others question what the Bible says about God's omnipotence. They believe that He does indeed love us and would like to take away all suffering and evil . . . but He is powerless to do so.

The apostle Peter wades into this question in this next section of his letter. It is actually a topic he has been addressing throughout as he has spoken to his readers—who themselves were enduring great suffering—about how to survive in a hostile world. He has emphasized the need to have a proper understanding of salvation . . . to know who they are and where they are headed. He has shown the wisdom of developing an attitude of submission and talked about the importance of acknowledging the lordship of Christ.

Now, the apostle Peter adds new context to the topic of earthly pain by helping his readers—and us—understand and appreciate the suffering of *Christ*. He notes, "Christ also suffered once for sins, the just for the unjust, that He might bring us to God" (1 Peter 3:18). If we keep our focus on what Jesus has done for us, we can survive and thrive in this world.

EXPLORING THE TEXT

Suffering for Right and Wrong (1 Peter 3:13–17)

¹³ And who is he who will harm you if you become followers of what is good? ¹⁴ But even if you should suffer for righteousness' sake, you are blessed. "And do not be afraid of their threats, nor be troubled." ¹⁵ But sanctify the Lord God in your hearts, and always be ready to

give a defense to everyone who asks you a reason for the hope that is in you, with meekness and fear; [16] having a good conscience, that when they defame you as evildoers, those who revile your good conduct in Christ may be ashamed. [17] For it is better, if it is the will of God, to suffer for doing good than for doing evil.

---

1. Peter transitions to the topic of suffering by asking his readers a rhetorical question: "Who is he who will harm you if you become followers of what is good?" (verse 13). Peter has an eternal focus here in mind and echoes the words of Jesus: "Do not fear those who kill the body . . . fear Him who is able to destroy both soul and body" (Matthew 10:28). What does Peter say in this respect about those who suffer for righteousness (see 1 Peter 3:13–14)?

_____

_____

_____

2. Peter wants his readers to understand their status before God in heaven does not mean they will escape threats, intimidation, and trouble. What are they to do instead of worrying about these things? What will be the result of such a "defense" (see verses 15–17)?

_____

_____

_____

The Example of Christ's Suffering (1 Peter 3:18–22)

[18] For Christ also suffered once for sins, the just for the unjust, that He might bring us to God, being put to death in the flesh but made alive by the Spirit, [19] by whom also He went and preached to the spirits

in prison, [20] who formerly were disobedient, when once the Divine longsuffering waited in the days of Noah, while the ark was being prepared, in which a few, that is, eight souls, were saved through water. [21] There is also an antitype which now saves us—baptism (not the removal of the filth of the flesh, but the answer of a good conscience toward God), through the resurrection of Jesus Christ, [22] who has gone into heaven and is at the right hand of God, angels and authorities and powers having been made subject to Him.

---

3. Peter's words in this next section are among the most difficult to interpret in the New Testament, but the key idea is that even Jesus, our example, suffered unjustly—so believers in Christ should not expect anything different. What does Peter say happened after Jesus was put to death in the flesh? Why is this critical for our faith (see verses 18–19)?

----

4. Scholars debate the identity of "the spirits in prison, who formerly were disobedient" (verses 19–20) to whom Jesus preached. This could refer to contemporaries of Noah or be a general reference to *all* righteous people who died before the coming of Christ. Regardless, the point is that Jesus suffered for *all* and now has all authority in heaven. How would this have given the readers of this letter hope as they suffered for Christ (see verses 20–22)?

GOING DEEPER

Peter is honest in telling his readers that they *will* confront people who will intend to do them harm. Jesus likewise warned His followers that there would be people in the world who would seek to "kill the body" (Matthew 10:28). There would come those who would seek to put an end to their lives because they professed that Jesus was the Messiah and was God. Shortly before His death, He took His disciples aside and gave further warning about what they could expect in the days ahead, as the following passage from the Gospel of John relates.

Jesus Warns and Comforts His Disciples (John 16:1–4)

¹ "These things I have spoken to you, that you should not be made to stumble. ² They will put you out of the synagogues; yes, the time is coming that whoever kills you will think that he offers God service. ³ And these things they will do to you because they have not known the Father nor Me. ⁴ But these things I have told you, that when the time comes, you may remember that I told you of them. "And these things I did not say to you at the beginning, because I was with you."

5. Jesus issued this warning so His disciples could prepare for the troubles that lay ahead—both after His death, which was imminent at this point, and for the rest of their lives. What specific trials did He imply they were going to face (see verses 1–2)?

_____

_____

_____

_____

6. Jesus' reference to being put out of the synagogues suggests that persecution would come from His followers' fellow Jews—the people

65

with whom they worshiped in the Temple. What would this sudden change in attitude reveal about the persecutors (see verses 3–4)?

_____

_____

_____

_____

_____

The Bible reveals that not even disciples like Peter or apostles like Paul were exempt from persecution, suffering, and hostility at the hands of those who intended to do them harm. Paul, for his part, endured more that his fair share of trials in life. In his letter to the church in Philippi, he acknowledged the pain he had endured, but he also recognized that his suffering connected him to Christ's righteousness. He actually *desired* to share in Jesus' suffering.

All for Christ (Philippians 3:7–11)

7 But what things were gain to me, these I have counted loss for Christ. 8 Yet indeed I also count all things loss for the excellence of the knowledge of Christ Jesus my Lord, for whom I have suffered the loss of all things, and count them as rubbish, that I may gain Christ 9 and be found in Him, not having my own righteousness, which is from the law, but that which is through faith in Christ, the righteousness which is from God by faith; 10 that I may know Him and the power of His resurrection, and the fellowship of His sufferings, being conformed to His death, 11 if, by any means, I may attain to the resurrection from the dead.

7. Scholars of the Bible believe that Paul was writing this letter to the Philippian believers from a Roman prison. How does the fact that he had been jailed for preaching the gospel lend credence and force to his words (see verses 7–8)?

_____

_____

_____

_____

8. Paul did not rely on his own righteousness or strength. How was he able to claim God's righteousness as well as the strength to endure suffering (see verses 9–11)?

_____

_____

_____

REVIEWING THE STORY

Peter wrote his letter to a group of believers who were wrestling with the problem of pain and suffering in this world. Peter does not dismiss their pain or even imply their situation will eventually be improved. Instead, he states they will be blessed when they suffer for righteousness and encourages them to be bold in sharing the truth of the gospel . . . in spite of the consequences. Peter then points to Christ as the ultimate example of what it means to suffer unjustly for righteousness' sake. The believers are to remember that because of what Christ endured, they will one day have an eternal home with God in heaven.

9. What does Peter say happens when we suffer for righteousness' sake (see 1 Peter 3:14)?

_____

_____

_____

10. For what should we be ready to give a defense (see 1 Peter 3:15–16)?

11. For whom did Jesus choose to suffer (see 1 Peter 3:18)?

12. By what means are we saved from our sins (see 1 Peter 3:21)?

APPLYING THE MESSAGE

13. What good has God brought out of some of the painful moments in your life?

14. How has God used trials to help you to grow and develop in your faith?

REFLECTING ON THE MEANING

In this passage, Peter draws a link between Christ's suffering and our suffering as believers. He emphasizes the *pain* that Jesus endured, reminding them that Christ was "put to death in the flesh" through an excruciating execution on a Roman cross. He calls out the *paradox* of Jesus' suffering, reminding his readers that He was the only sinless person to ever live. He then points to the *purpose* of Christ's suffering—so that He might bring us to God.

When we likewise suffer for the sake of the gospel, we can realize three great purposes in our lives. *First, our suffering secures a greater ministry.* When we look at our suffering, we always view it in a negative sense. We see financial pressures, family troubles, and personal struggles as obstacles to our ministry. In reality, God might be using these things to open up new avenues of ministry. He may be using our brokenness to help us recognize brokenness in others. He may be preparing us to have the greatest influence we have ever had in our lives.

Second, our suffering sets us apart for greater witness and influence. Peter told the believers to "always be ready to give a defense to everyone who asks you a reason for the hope that is in you" (1 Peter 3:15). If we follow Jesus' example in responding to suffering, *people will notice.* They will be curious. Some will study us from a distance, perhaps without our realizing it. Others will ask questions. Their attitudes may range from amazement to skepticism, but the questions will be the same: "What makes you different?" Suddenly, we have an opportunity to talk about the reason for our hope—one we would not have had without suffering.

Third, our suffering sends us to glory in the presence of the Lord. Peter looks squarely at the worst-case scenario and asks, "What's so bad about it?" The worst possible outcome of our suffering is that we will be released from our body to live in the presence of Almighty God for eternity. The very *worst* thing that could ever happen to us is the *best* thing that could ever happen. As Paul put it, "For to me, to live is Christ, and to die is gain" (Philippians 1:21).

The reality of this life is that we *will* face trials, toils, and troubles. The question is whether we will allow those challenges to wear us down or whether we will allow God to use them to build our ministry, our witness to others, and our faith in Him. As we fix our eyes on Christ and allow Him to change our mindset, we can see the good in even the worst situation.

JOURNALING YOUR RESPONSE

How have you seen God use your suffering or pain as a witness to others?

ADOPTING THE MIND OF CHRIST

1 Peter 4:1–19

GETTING STARTED

How do you prepare yourself mentally for times of trial and adversity?

_____

_____

_____

_____

_____

_____

_____

_____

_____

_____

_____

SETTING THE STAGE

History reveals the persecution of the early church occurred sporadically and in localized areas from the start. As noted in the last session, Saul was among the early persecutors before his life was transformed and he became known as the apostle Paul (see Acts 8:1–3). The first organized Roman persecution of Christians took place in AD 64 under the reign of Nero, who needed a scapegoat for the Great Fire of Rome that he himself had likely ordered in that year.

Both Peter and Paul would lose their lives during this Neronian persecution, as would many of the original recipients of their letters. The danger was real. This is why Peter wanted to ensure the believers had the proper mindset about their trials. In the same way, while we will likely never face the prospect of martyrdom, we will face hostility, ridicule, and scorn, and it's critically important that we know how to deal with such opposition.

Peter drew a comparison in his previous chapter between the suffering endured by Jesus during His time on earth and the suffering endured by Jesus' followers. He emphasized the importance of fully acknowledging and appreciating Christ's suffering. After all, every bit of the agony Christ faced was on their behalf. In this chapter, he takes the concept one step further, stating that believers are to have "the same mind" as Christ. The key to enduring suffering, and even thriving in the midst of it, is to approach it with the mindset of Christ.

Now, it should be noted that Peter's words of wisdom apply only to the suffering believers face for doing *good*. They have no application to the trouble we endure as evildoers. If we face suffering for something wrong we have done, we are only getting what we deserve. Peter is not talking about reaping what we sow but about the type of adversity that comes with no relative purpose that we can discern—suffering that is uninvited by us.

EXPLORING THE TEXT

Living for Christ (1 Peter 4:1–11)

> [1] Therefore, since Christ suffered for us in the flesh, arm yourselves also with the same mind, for he who has suffered in the flesh has ceased from sin, [2] that he no longer should live the rest of his time in

the flesh for the lusts of men, but for the will of God. ³ For we have spent enough of our past lifetime in doing the will of the Gentiles— when we walked in lewdness, lusts, drunkenness, revelries, drinking parties, and abominable idolatries. ⁴ In regard to these, they think it strange that you do not run with them in the same flood of dissipation, speaking evil of you. ⁵ They will give an account to Him who is ready to judge the living and the dead. ⁶ For this reason the gospel was preached also to those who are dead, that they might be judged according to men in the flesh, but live according to God in the spirit.

⁷ But the end of all things is at hand; therefore be serious and watchful in your prayers. ⁸ And above all things have fervent love for one another, for "love will cover a multitude of sins." ⁹ Be hospitable to one another without grumbling. ¹⁰ As each one has received a gift, minister it to one another, as good stewards of the manifold grace of God. ¹¹ If anyone speaks, let him speak as the oracles of God. If anyone ministers, let him do it as with the ability which God supplies, that in all things God may be glorified through Jesus Christ, to whom belong the glory and the dominion forever and ever. Amen.

---

1. Peter makes the astonishing statement that those who suffer in the flesh have "ceased from sin" (verse 1). The idea is that suffering can serve as a form of a "refining fire" that causes us to draw closer to God and evaluate whether we have turned our backs on our former ways of living. What does Peter call out about his readers' former ways of life? What does he say will happen to those who speak evil of them (see verses 1–6)?

2. Peter's comment that the "the end of all things is at hand" refers to the second coming of Christ and the judgment that will follow. The idea is that such a prospect should cause believers to narrow their priorities. What are some of the things that Peter states should take precedence in their lives? What is the ultimate goal of their service (see verses 7–11)?

Suffering for God's Glory (1 Peter 4:12–19)

¹² Beloved, do not think it strange concerning the fiery trial which is to try you, as though some strange thing happened to you; ¹³ but rejoice to the extent that you partake of Christ's sufferings, that when His glory is revealed, you may also be glad with exceeding joy. ¹⁴ If you are reproached for the name of Christ, blessed are you, for the Spirit of glory and of God rests upon you. On their part He is blasphemed, but on your part He is glorified. ¹⁵ But let none of you suffer as a murderer, a thief, an evildoer, or as a busybody in other people's matters. ¹⁶ Yet if anyone suffers as a Christian, let him not be ashamed, but let him glorify God in this matter.

¹⁷ For the time has come for judgment to begin at the house of God; and if it begins with us first, what will be the end of those who do not obey the gospel of God? ¹⁸ Now

"If the righteous one is scarcely saved,
Where will the ungodly and the sinner appear?"

¹⁹ Therefore let those who suffer according to the will of God commit their souls to Him in doing good, as to a faithful Creator.

3. Peter does not dismiss or downplay the painful effects of suffering in his readers' lives. But rather than being shocked or surprised by it, they are to rejoice in it. What reasons does he give as to why they can rejoice when they partake in Jesus' sufferings? What is his caveat for those who are suffering as a result of their own wrong actions (see verses 12–16)?

4. Peter draws on the words of Proverbs 11:31 to contrast the judgment taking place in "the house of God" (through conviction of sin) to the judgment that will take place for those "who do not obey the gospel of God." How might this have helped Peter's readers to reframe their sufferings? What should they do in their suffering (see verses 17–19)?

GOING DEEPER

The idea that God uses trials and adversity might be uncomfortable for us to accept, but that teaching appears frequently in both the Old and New Testaments. For example, in the book of Proverbs we read, "Do not despise the chastening of the LORD, nor detest His correction; for whom the LORD loves He corrects" (3:11–12). In the letter of Hebrews, the author goes into greater detail about the discipline of God, reinforcing many of Peter's points in this section.

The Discipline of God (Hebrews 12:3–8)

[3] For consider Him who endured such hostility from sinners against Himself, lest you become weary and discouraged in your souls. [4] You have not yet resisted to bloodshed, striving against sin. [5] And you have forgotten the exhortation which speaks to you as to sons:

> "My son, do not despise the chastening of the LORD,
> Nor be discouraged when you are rebuked by Him;
> [6] For whom the LORD loves He chastens,
> And scourges every son whom He receives."

[7] If you endure chastening, God deals with you as with sons; for what son is there whom a father does not chasten?   But if you are without chastening, of which all have become partakers, then you are illegitimate and not sons.

---

5. The author of Hebrews, much like Peter, calls on believers to consider the example of Christ in their sufferings. Jesus also "endured such hostility from sinners," just as they are facing. What should their mindset be as they confront such trials (see verses 3–6)?

----

6. What is the promise for those who endure "chastening" (see verse 7)? How do the words in this passage align with Peter's message about enduring through trials?

_____

_____

_____

_____

_____

_____

_____

_____

_____

_____

Renew Your Spiritual Vitality (Hebrews 12:9–13)

⁹ Furthermore, we have had human fathers who corrected us, and we paid them respect. Shall we not much more readily be in subjection to the Father of spirits and live? ¹⁰ For they indeed for a few days chastened us as seemed best to them, but He for our profit, that we may be partakers of His holiness. ¹¹ Now no chastening seems to be joyful for the present, but painful; nevertheless, afterward it yields the peaceable fruit of righteousness to those who have been trained by it.

¹² Therefore strengthen the hands which hang down, and the feeble knees, ¹³ and make straight paths for your feet, so that what is lame may not be dislocated, but rather be healed.

7. The author emphasizes his point by calling his readers to consider the discipline they have received from their human fathers. But what is the key difference between the discipline we receive from parents and the discipline that God provides (see verses 9–10)?

8. The writer of Hebrews, just like Peter, does not downplay the painful nature of suffering. Nevertheless, what does he say it will yield (see verses 11–12)?

Reviewing the Story

The first-century believers to whom Peter was writing faced the real prospect of martyrdom for their faith. Peter does not dismiss this reality but encourages his readers to change their mindset when it comes to viewing their trials. He urges them to look to the example Jesus set when He faced suffering. He tells them to leave behind their former way of living. He reminds them that Jesus' return is at hand and they need to continue pursuing a holy life. He concludes by stressing that those who deny Christ will ultimately face judgment for their sins.

9. What should we cease doing if we are truly following Jesus' example (see 1 Peter 4:1–2)?

10. How are we to relate to other believers and use our gifts (see 1 Peter 4:9–10)?

11. Why are we able to rejoice when we suffer for doing good (see 1 Peter 4:13)?

12. What should be our attitude when we suffer for Christ (see 1 Peter 4:16)?

Applying the Message

13. How have times of adversity caused you to reflect on your attitudes and behaviors?

_____

_____

_____

_____

_____

_____

14. What does it mean for you to live as if "the end of all things is at hand"?

_____

_____

_____

_____

_____

_____

Reflecting on the Meaning

There is a tendency among believers today to diminish the suffering of Jesus. We think of Him suffering as the "Son of God" but not as a flesh-and-blood human. But Peter states that "Christ suffered for us in the flesh" (1 Peter 4:1). He knew what it felt like to be betrayed, shed tears, and experience pain. We can thus identify with Christ because He experienced everything that we experience. Peter calls out four points for us to consider as it relates to this truth.

First, the potential of our identification with Christ. Peter writes that "he who has suffered in the flesh has ceased from sin" (verse 1). In the original

Greek, the word translated *ceased* is closer in meaning to the word *released*. Jesus suffered in the flesh, died for our sin, and afterward was *released* from the responsibility for sin. The penalty was paid for all humankind for all time. Peter says this same freedom is available to us! By identifying with Christ and His suffering, we are able to be set free from sin and can lead our lives apart from it.

Second, the power of our identification of Christ. Peter writes that since Jesus suffered for us in the flesh, we can "arm [ourselves] also with the same mind" (verse 1). In other words, there is a spiritual action we can take in response to Jesus' sacrifice for us. We can use what we know about the death of Christ—and how He approached His death—in the battles we face. The word translated as *mind* in this verse is literally the word *thought*. We can *arm* ourselves with the same thought pattern that Jesus had when He suffered and died.

Third, the peril of our identification with Christ. Peter warns that those who do not know Christ will "think it strange" that we do not participate in their ungodly behaviors and will end up "speaking evil" of (verse 4). When people find out that we are living for Christ, they are going to abuse us, say bad things about us, put us down, and make us look small in the eyes of others. However, knowing this will enable us to have a Christlike mindset and will allow us to prepare for these hardships by studying Jesus' example.

Fourth, the promise of our identification with Christ. Peter warns that those who speak evil of us "will give an account to Him who is ready to judge the living and the dead" (verse 5). God promises that our suffering on this earth is not the end of the story. A day is coming when God will judge those who have denied Him and reward those who serve Him.

Peter tells us to arm ourselves with these truths so we can adopt the mind of Christ and stand strong in the face persecution, suffering, and trials. In this way, when people attack us, they will see there is something inside us so powerful that it makes their attacks pointless. As Peter states, "On their part [Christ] is blasphemed, but on your part He is glorified" (verse 14). Our trials will point people to Christ . . . and God will bless us as a result.

JOURNALING YOUR RESPONSE

How could adopting Christ's mindset help you in any trials you are currently facing?

COMBATING THE ENEMY

1 Peter 5:1–14

GETTING STARTED

Why is it important for Christians to recognize the devil is real and at work in the world?

_____

_____

_____

_____

_____

_____

_____

_____

_____

_____

_____

_____

_____

_____

_____

_____

SETTING THE STAGE

If you are an experienced letter writer, you know that the most important message should be saved for the end. If there is something you really want your readers to remember, you include it just before your signature. Usually, this is prefaced with a phrase such as, "and don't forget." The New Testament writers understood this technique. The apostle Paul often wrapped up his correspondence in a way that captured the gist of the entire letter but also drove home the key point. Peter does the same thing in this final section . . . and what he says is crucial.

Peter's final "don't forget" message to his recipients comes in two parts. First, he includes a special word to those who minister. He reminds them of the salient principles that hold ministry together. He encourages them to be faithful, caring, humble, and honest in their oversight of "the flock" and to serve as a good example. Now, these words actually apply to *all* believers, for all faithful followers of Christ have been called in some way to minister to others.

Peter's second "don't forget" message to his readers is that they are up against a crafty enemy who wants to devour them. They must stay vigilant because they are fighting in a *war* . . . and there are no Geneva Convention rules for this engagement. However, even though their enemy is invisible, he is not unidentifiable. He has tendencies they can observe. Knowing these tendencies will allow them—and us—to devise strategies for victory.

Peter's closing takeaway is that we must never be lulled into a state of slumber. We should never underestimate the seriousness of our battles or the desperation of our enemy. We need to know what to expect in the heat of battle and engage with a sense of urgency. The victory is ours in Christ, and we have allies in the fight . . . but the battles must still be fought.

EXPLORING THE TEXT

Instructions for Elders and the Flock (1 Peter 5:1–7)

¹ The elders who are among you I exhort, I who am a fellow elder and a witness of the sufferings of Christ, and also a partaker of the glory that will be revealed: ² Shepherd the flock of God which is among you, serving as overseers, not by compulsion but willingly,

not for dishonest gain but eagerly; [3] nor as being lords over those entrusted to you, but being examples to the flock; [4] and when the Chief Shepherd appears, you will receive the crown of glory that does not fade away.

[5] Likewise you younger people, submit yourselves to your elders. Yes, all of you be submissive to one another, and be clothed with humility, for

> "God resists the proud,
> But gives grace to the humble."

[6] Therefore humble yourselves under the mighty hand of God, that He may exalt you in due time, [7] casting all your care upon Him, for He cares for you.

---

1. Peter ends his letter with remarks directed at three groups in the church: (1) the elders, (2) the younger members, and (3) all the believers. He states that he is qualified to speak to all three groups because he is a fellow elder who has witnessed Jesus' suffering and glory and is no stranger to Satan's attacks. How does he advise the elders to lead? What role does he want them to play in helping the flock to follow after the Chief Shepherd (see verses 1–4)?

2. Peter's words to the "younger people" in the churches emphasize a theme of submission that he has employed throughout in the letter. The younger members are to honor and respect the older and wiser members of their community. Why does Peter stress that it is important for them to be submissive and practice humility (see verses 5–7)?

_____

_____

_____

_____

_____

_____

_____

_____

_____

Resist the Devil (1 Peter 5:8–14)

⁸ Be sober, be vigilant; because your adversary the devil walks about like a roaring lion, seeking whom he may devour. ⁹ Resist him, steadfast in the faith, knowing that the same sufferings are experienced by your brotherhood in the world. ¹⁰ But may the God of all grace, who called us to His eternal glory by Christ Jesus, after you have suffered a while, perfect, establish, strengthen, and settle you. ¹¹ To Him be the glory and the dominion forever and ever. Amen.

¹² By Silvanus, our faithful brother as I consider him, I have written to you briefly, exhorting and testifying that this is the true grace of God in which you stand.

¹³ She who is in Babylon, elect together with you, greets you; and so does Mark my son. ¹⁴ Greet one another with a kiss of love.

Peace to you all who are in Christ Jesus. Amen.

3. Peter has encouraged his readers to submit to God and entrust their lives to His care. Even in a world filled with evil, suffering, and persecution, they can know they are under the protection of a sovereign God. However, they still have an active role to play. What does Peter warn about the foe they face? How can they combat him (see verses 8–9)?

_____

_____

_____

_____

_____

_____

4. Peter closes with a prayer and greetings from Silvanus (Silas), the believers "in Babylon" (Rome), and Mark. What does Peter ask God to do for his readers (see verses 10–11)?

_____

_____

_____

_____

_____

GOING DEEPER

Peter warned his readers they were at *war* against a real enemy. Jesus likewise explained to His followers they were up against a foe who was "a murderer from the beginning" and a thief who "does not come except to steal, and to kill and destroy" (John 8:44; 10:10). Other authors of the New Testament pointed also out the devil's treachery and called on believers to remain vigilant. In James' letter, he offers a spiritual battle plan for victory. In Paul's letter to the church in Ephesus, he instructs believers to "suit up" with God's armor to do battle against the devil.

Draw Near to God (James 4:7–10)

> ⁷ Therefore submit to God. Resist the devil and he will flee from you. ⁸ Draw near to God and He will draw near to you. Cleanse your hands, you sinners; and purify your hearts, you double-minded. ⁹ Lament and mourn and weep! Let your laughter be turned to mourning and your joy to gloom. ¹⁰ Humble yourselves in the sight of the Lord, and He will lift you up.

5. The phrase "submit to God" means to surrender to Him as a conquering King. What does placing ourselves under His authority give us the power to do? What does James promise that God will do as we choose to submit and draw near to Him (see verses 7–8)?

_____

_____

_____

_____

_____

6. The instructions to "lament and mourn and weep" call believers to put aside any carefree attitudes regarding sin and recognize they are in a spiritual battle. What does James say will happen when we humble ourselves and mourn in true repentance (see verses 9–10)?

_____

_____

_____

_____

The Armor of God (Ephesians 6:10–20)

[10] Finally, my brethren, be strong in the Lord and in the power of His might. [11] Put on the whole armor of God, that you may be able to stand against the wiles of the devil. [12] For we do not wrestle against flesh and blood, but against principalities, against powers, against the rulers of the darkness of this age, against spiritual hosts of wickedness in the heavenly places. [13] Therefore take up the whole armor of God, that you may be able to withstand in the evil day, and having done all, to stand.

[14] Stand therefore, having girded your waist with truth, having put on the breastplate of righteousness, [15] and having shod your feet with the preparation of the gospel of peace; [16] above all, taking the shield of faith with which you will be able to quench all the fiery darts of the wicked one. [17] And take the helmet of salvation, and the sword of the Spirit, which is the word of God; [18] praying always with all prayer and supplication in the Spirit, being watchful to this end with all perseverance and supplication for all the saints— [19] and for me, that utterance may be given to me, that I may open my mouth boldly to make known the mystery of the gospel, [20] for which I am an ambassador in chains; that in it I may speak boldly, as I ought to speak.

7. The apostle Paul encourages believers in Christ to resist the devil by putting on "the whole armor of God." How does he describe the forces in the spiritual realm that are against us? What happens when we put on God's armor (see verses 10–13)?

_____

_____

_____

_____

_____

8. The armor that God has made available to us includes truth, righteousness, the gospel, faith, and salvation. When we are equipped with each of these attributes, we are able to stand against the enemy's attacks. What is the offensive weapon that God has provided to us? What else does Paul say we must do to fight back against the devil (see verses 17–20)?

_____

_____

_____

_____

_____

REVIEWING THE STORY

Peter closes his letter with a few instructions on how church elders can best shepherd their "flocks" and with an admonition for the younger believers to submit to their authority and not be proud. He reminds all believers that they must be sober and vigilant because they are engaged in a spiritual battle against a foe that seeks to devour them like a roaring lion. He encourages them to resist the devil, remain steadfast in their faith, and remember that the suffering they are enduring is being experienced by all believers in the world.

9. How does Peter describe himself to the elders in the church (see 1 Peter 5:1)?

_____

_____

_____

_____

_____

10. What happens when we humble ourselves before God
(see 1 Peter 5:6–7)?

_____

_____

_____

_____

_____

_____

_____

11. What does God do for us in the midst of our suffering and struggle
(see 1 Peter 5:10)?

_____

_____

_____

_____

_____

_____

12. What do Peter and Silas testify to the believers (see 1 Peter 5:12)?

_____

_____

_____

_____

_____

_____

APPLYING THE MESSAGE

13. What struggles do you tend to have when it comes to submitting to God in humility?

_____

_____

_____

_____

_____

_____

_____

14. What are some effective strategies that you have developed for resisting the devil?

_____

_____

_____

_____

_____

_____

_____

_____

REFLECTING ON THE MEANING

As we have discussed, the apostle Peter wrote his first letter to believers who were scattered throughout the Roman Empire. These Christians were living under the rule of Emperor Nero, who had sought to make them a scapegoat for the misfortunes that had befallen Rome. Peter reminds these believers under siege that their battle is not with flesh-and-blood but with a spiritual adversary that seeks their ultimate (and eternal) destruction.

As he closes his letter, he sends these believers off with three important strategies to fight this war.

First, believers must adopt the attitude of a warrior. Peter tells followers of Christ to "be sober [and] be vigilant" (1 Peter 5:8). The word *sober* means to see our enemy for what he really is. The term *vigilant* means to always be watching so that we can spot how Satan is working. Peter says our enemy is like a "roaring lion" who prowls the earth, collecting evidence he can take to the Lord to discredit us. He is our accuser! He knows that he cannot take away our spiritual life, so he seeks to destroy our influence, credibility, testimony, and trust in God.

Second, believers must practice the actions of a warrior. Peter's guidance is to "resist" the devil and remain "steadfast in the faith" (see verse 9). Notice the instruction is not to *flee* the devil but to *withstand* his attacks. There is no sense in running from the devil—we cannot abandon the battlefield. This is why Paul instructs us to "put on the whole armor of God" (Ephesians 6:10) and then lists each piece of spiritual armor (see verses 14–17). We keep Satan from making inroads in our lives by using that which God has given us to defeat him.

Third, believers must recognize the allies of a warrior. Peter reminds his readers that "the same sufferings" are being experienced by their "brotherhood in the world" (1 Peter 5:9). One of Satan's strategies is to make us think no one else is facing the attacks that we are facing. But Peter reminds us that we have allies in the fight. We are not alone. In fact, God never intended us to face Satan's attacks by ourselves. We have brothers and sisters out there who will put their arms around us if we are vulnerable enough to let them know we are at war.

Peter closes his letter by stating that as we adopt the *attitude* and *actions of* a warrior, and recognize our *allies* in the fight, the Lord will "perfect, establish, strengthen, and settle" each of us (verse 10). These are the characteristics of spiritual maturity—the traits that set us apart from the rest of the world. But this spiritual maturity will only come after we are *engaged* in the fight. God will use our battles to transform us into the people whom He wants us to be.

JOURNALING YOUR RESPONSE

What are some ways that you have leaned on your Christian allies in the past?

LEADING AN EXCEPTIONAL LIFE

2 Peter 1:1–15

GETTING STARTED

How would you describe what it means to lead an exceptional life?

_____

_____

_____

_____

_____

_____

_____

_____

_____

_____

SETTING THE STAGE

One of the inescapable truths of Scripture is that God does not work in half measures. He never calls His followers to be just ordinary. He is not satisfied if they exert average effort in following after Him. No, God desires for His people to lead *exceptional* lives—lives that exhibit sacrifice, diligence, commitment, and genuine love for one another. Often, He will call His followers to lead such lives in times of difficulty, challenge, and chaos. As Jesus said, "In the world you will have tribulation; but be of good cheer, I have overcome the world" (John 16:33).

The recipients of Peter's second letter were no strangers to leading exceptional lives for God in the midst of tribulation. (In fact, they were likely the same group of believers to whom he had written his first letter.) These believers were facing increased suffering and persecution at the hands of Roman authorities, and their misery on earth was causing them to look forward to the second coming of Christ. Yet their understanding of this event was shaky at best, and this vulnerability was making them susceptible to false teachers who had infiltrated their communities. These outside influencers were causing great dissension among the believers.

So, Peter writes his second letter to again encourage them in their suffering, to address their concerns about Jesus' return, and to point out the error in the messages they were receiving from the false teachers. As we will discover in this lesson, he sets the tone from the start, emphasizing the need for the believers to remain diligent in their journey with Christ. He desires for them to stay engaged with life and not just wait for the day it would "all be over."

God wants the same for us today. In times of uncertainty and struggle, our tendency is often to check out and just coast through life. But we have to remember that God has not called us to an ordinary existence. He wants us to be continually engaged with the work that He has given us to do. When we are, we find that are able to take full advantage of the opportunities that He provides to make a difference in this world and lead fruitful lives.

EXPLORING THE TEXT

The Path to Spiritual Growth (2 Peter 1:1–8)

¹ Simon Peter, a bondservant and apostle of Jesus Christ,

To those who have obtained like precious faith with us by the righteousness of our God and Savior Jesus Christ:

² Grace and peace be multiplied to you in the knowledge of God and of Jesus our Lord, ³ as His divine power has given to us all things that pertain to life and godliness, through the knowledge of Him who called us by glory and virtue, ⁴ by which have been given to us exceedingly great and precious promises, that through these you may be partakers of the divine nature, having escaped the corruption that is in the world through lust.

⁵ But also for this very reason, giving all diligence, add to your faith virtue, to virtue knowledge, ⁶ to knowledge self-control, to self-control perseverance, to perseverance godliness, ⁷ to godliness brotherly kindness, and to brotherly kindness love. ⁸ For if these things are yours and abound, you will be neither barren nor unfruitful in the knowledge of our Lord Jesus Christ.

---

1. Peter opens his letter by citing his credentials as "a bondservant and apostle of Jesus Christ" (verse 1), which was a typical way of stating that he had the authority to offer instruction to the churches. He then immediately reminds his readers of the call they have received from God to lead exceptional, holy, and fruitful lives. What does Peter say God's divine power has enabled them to do? What else have they received from God (see verses 2–4)?

_____

_____

_____

_____

_____

_____

_____

_____

_____

2. Peter notes that God has provided the believers with everything they need to lead an exceptional life—beginning with their faith. How are they to build on their faith to grow in Christ? What happens when these traits abound in their lives (see verses 5–8)?

_____

_____

_____

_____

_____

_____

_____

_____

_____

_____

A Call for Diligence (2 Peter 1:9–15)

9 For he who lacks these things is shortsighted, even to blindness, and has forgotten that he was cleansed from his old sins. 10 Therefore, brethren, be even more diligent to make your call and election sure, for if you do these things you will never stumble; 11 for so an entrance will be supplied to you abundantly into the everlasting kingdom of our Lord and Savior Jesus Christ.

12 For this reason I will not be negligent to remind you always of these things, though you know and are established in the present truth. 13 Yes, I think it is right, as long as I am in this tent, to stir you up by reminding you, 14 knowing that shortly I must put off my tent, just as our Lord Jesus Christ showed me. 15 Moreover I will be careful to ensure that you always have a reminder of these things after my decease.

3. Peter warns that those who do not seek to live out the godly traits he has just outlined are walking in spiritual blindness and have forgotten what Christ has done for them. What does he instead call them to do? What will they receive if they do (see verses 9–11)?

_____

_____

_____

_____

_____

_____

4. Peter acknowledges that his readers are already "well established" in these truths that he has just discussed, but he also recognizes that his time on earth is coming to an end. What does he say he wants to do with his remaining days (see verses 12–15)?

_____

_____

_____

_____

_____

_____

Going Deeper

Peter opens his second letter with the aim of helping his readers pursue the course that God has set for them and to strive to lead godly lives. The apostle Paul frequently urged his readers to do the same. In his first letter to the believers in Corinth, he draws on the analogy of a runner to depict what it means to strive for the "prize" that God has set before them. In his second letter to Timothy, which scholars believe to be the last epistle written before his death, he urges believers to present themselves as approved workers before God.

Striving for a Crown (1 Corinthians 9:24–27)

24 Do you not know that those who run in a race all run, but one receives the prize? Run in such a way that you may obtain it. 25 And everyone who competes for the prize is temperate in all things. Now they do it to obtain a perishable crown, but we for an imperishable crown. 26 Therefore I run thus: not with uncertainty. Thus I fight: not as one who beats the air. 27 But I discipline my body and bring it into subjection, lest, when I have preached to others, I myself should become disqualified.

5. Paul's use of the word "temperate" (verse 25) refers to Roman athletes who had to train for ten months before they were allowed to compete. In using this word, what does he want his reader to understand about the exceptional life God has for them (see verses 24–25)?

6. It is essential for athletes to discipline their bodies in order to compete at their highest level. Why is it important for Christians to likewise bring their bodies into subjection—under the control of their minds—in order to serve God at the highest level (see verses 26–27)?

_____

_____

_____

_____

_____

_____

_____

_____

Be Strong in Grace (2 Timothy 2:11–16)

¹¹ This is a faithful saying:

> For if we died with Him,
> We shall also live with Him.
> ¹² If we endure,
> We shall also reign with Him.
> If we deny Him,
> He also will deny us.
> ¹³ If we are faithless,
> He remains faithful;
> He cannot deny Himself.

¹⁴ Remind them of these things, charging them before the Lord not to strive about words to no profit, to the ruin of the hearers. ¹⁵ Be diligent to present yourself approved to God, a worker who

does not need to be ashamed, rightly dividing the word of truth. ¹⁶ But shun profane and idle babblings, for they will increase to more ungodliness.

---

7. Paul quotes to Timothy a "faithful saying" or early Christian hymn that was popular in his day. What inspiration and encouragement does this offer to believers who are seeking to lead exceptional and fruitful lives for Christ (see verses 11–13)?

_____

_____

_____

_____

_____

8. Paul urges Timothy to not engage in words with "no profit" and to look to God for approval. What will happen if he remains diligent in this pursuit (see verses 14–16)?

_____

_____

_____

_____

_____

REVIEWING THE STORY

Peter begins his second letter by explaining that God has given believers in Christ everything they need to live a godly, purpose-filled, exceptional life. He reminds his readers that they are partakers in God's divine nature and have escaped the corruption of the world. He encourages them to be diligent in growing in faith, virtue, knowledge, self-control, perseverance, godliness, brotherly kindness, and love. Peter recognizes that his time on earth is running short. But he wants to remind the believers of these truths so they will not stumble in their faith.

9. What have believers in Christ escaped (see 2 Peter 1:4)?

_____

_____

_____

_____

10. What kind of life will a person lead who abounds in faith, virtue, knowledge, self-control, perseverance, godliness, brotherly kindness, and love (see 2 Peter 1:8)?

_____

_____

_____

_____

11. What enables a believer in Christ to never stumble (see 2 Peter 1:10)?

_____

_____

_____

_____

_____

12. What did Peter want to ensure would happen after his death (see 2 Peter 1:15)?

_____

_____

_____

_____

APPLYING THE MESSAGE

13. How are you growing in faith, virtue, knowledge, and self-control?

_____

_____

_____

_____

14. How are you growing in the traits of perseverance, godliness, kindness, and love?

_____

_____

_____

_____

REFLECTING ON THE MEANING

Notice the progression of living an exceptional life that Peter outlines in this opening section of his letter. We begin with our *faith* in Christ. We add *virtue*, which is our courage to do the right thing at all times. We add *knowledge,* or our understanding of God's Word. We add *self-control,* which is the practice of choosing what we do, say, and think. We add *perseverance,* which involves pushing past obstacles that derail our progress. We add *godliness,* which means to have reverence for the God we serve. Finally, to these we add *brotherly kindness* and *love.*

Peter states that when we pursue these traits with diligence, three things will happen that will set us on a course to leading an exceptional life. First, *we will have stability in the way we live.* Character is the result of persistent action. As we diligently pursue the Christian life, old and unhelpful habits will fall away, and new and profitable habits will grow. We will be more resistant to the ups and downs of life. We discover an inner strength that takes us through situations we never believed we could endure as we help others along the way.

Second, we will have vitality in our Christian lives. The word *vitality* refers to the abundant mental and physical energy that people tend to lose as they get older. It is the ability to spring out of bed in the morning to greet the new day—the strength to embrace change and not fear it. If we look at the lives of the mature saints we know, we see that kind of vitality, even deep into their golden years. Wouldn't it be great to grow with a grace like that? These qualities, lived out diligently, can make that happen.

Third, we have reality in our Christian lives. Peter states that we "will be neither barren nor unfruitful in the knowledge of our Lord Jesus Christ" (2 Peter 1:8). We will know God's truth deeply and witness it bearing fruit all around us. We will be involved in the real world, connecting the truth of the gospel to the needs of the people we see. Some claim that faith is a fantasy world to escape the problems of the day, but Peter says that when we have diligence in developing our walk with Christ, we become more real than we have ever been before.

God has given us everything we need to develop a passionate, focused, and diligent life. We don't need any more information or another revelation—we only need to open God's Word. It is up to us to take what we have received and give it back to God. It is time for us to lead the extraordinary lives that will bring honor to His name and strength to our lives.

JOURNALING YOUR RESPONSE

What next step is God calling you to take to lead an extraordinary life?

EMBRACING THE TRUTH

2 Peter 1:16–2:11

GETTING STARTED

How do you determine whether someone is telling you the truth?

SETTING THE STAGE

What is the truth? Sadly, the question has never been more difficult to answer. Social media often obliterates the lines between real and fake. Apps allow us to filter and distort our appearance. Video technology makes it possible to realistically portray things that never happened as actual events. Websites run misleading headlines just to generate more traffic.

Where does that leave us? Armed with our intuition, investigative skills, knowledge, and personal experience, we are left to sort through the barrage of messages that claim to be true. We have to determine which sources of information are trustworthy . . . and which are not. The same process applies when we are discerning *spiritual* truth. We cannot just accept everything we hear as truth. We have to decide which sources of information we are going to trust.

The recipients of Peter's second letter were caught in this dilemma. False teachers had appeared in their midst who were proclaiming a message contrary to the doctrine they had received. Some of these individuals were evidently claiming that Peter and the other genuine apostles were just telling "cunningly devised fables" when it came to Christ (2 Peter 1:16). These critics of the gospel were confusing the believers and casting doubt on the Christian faith.

Peter meets these opponents head-on—and not just as a writer of the Bible, but also as an eyewitness to the events he has described. Peter knew the truth about Jesus because He was *there* as Jesus' ministry unfolded. He was present at the transfiguration, the Last Supper, and the crucifixion. He walked on water with Jesus. He had breakfast with Him after His resurrection. Peter knew what could and could not be trusted. In this passage, he helps his readers discern what is false so they can embrace the truth that is theirs in Christ.

EXPLORING THE TEXT

The Trustworthy Prophetic Word (2 Peter 1:16–21)

16 For we did not follow cunningly devised fables when we made known to you the power and coming of our Lord Jesus Christ, but were eyewitnesses of His majesty. 17 For He received from God the

Father honor and glory when such a voice came to Him from the Excellent Glory: "This is My beloved Son, in whom I am well pleased." [18] And we heard this voice which came from heaven when we were with Him on the holy mountain.

[19] And so we have the prophetic word confirmed, which you do well to heed as a light that shines in a dark place, until the day dawns and the morning star rises in your hearts; [20] knowing this first, that no prophecy of Scripture is of any private interpretation, [21] for prophecy never came by the will of man, but holy men of God spoke as they were moved by the Holy Spirit.

---

1. Peter's words in this next section of his letter indicate that certain false teachers were calling his apostolic authority into question. They were claiming that Peter and the other apostles were merely relating "cunningly devised fables." How does Peter respond to these claims? What does he cite as the foundation for his authority (see verses 16–18)?

_____

_____

_____

_____

_____

_____

_____

_____

_____

_____

2. Peter continues to defend his apostolic authority by showing that his message originated with God. Just as God inspired the Old Testament prophets, so He has inspired Peter to proclaim the message of Christ.

What does Peter say this "prophetic word" will do in the believers' lives if they heed it? Whom does he cite as the source of this message (see verses 19–21)?

_____

_____

_____

_____

_____

_____

_____

_____

_____

Destructive Doctrines (2 Peter 2:1–11)

¹ But there were also false prophets among the people, even as there will be false teachers among you, who will secretly bring in destructive heresies, even denying the Lord who bought them, and bring on themselves swift destruction. ² And many will follow their destructive ways, because of whom the way of truth will be blasphemed. ³ By covetousness they will exploit you with deceptive words; for a long time their judgment has not been idle, and their destruction does not slumber.

⁴ For if God did not spare the angels who sinned, but cast them down to hell and delivered them into chains of darkness, to be reserved for judgment; ⁵ and did not spare the ancient world, but saved Noah, one of eight people, a preacher of righteousness, bringing in the flood on the world of the ungodly; ⁶ and turning the cities of Sodom and Gomorrah into ashes, condemned them to destruction, making them an example to those who afterward would

live ungodly; ⁷ and delivered righteous Lot, who was oppressed by the filthy conduct of the wicked ⁸ (for that righteous man, dwelling among them, tormented his righteous soul from day to day by seeing and hearing their lawless deeds)— ⁹ then the Lord knows how to deliver the godly out of temptations and to reserve the unjust under punishment for the day of judgment, ¹⁰ and especially those who walk according to the flesh in the lust of uncleanness and despise authority. They are presumptuous, self-willed. They are not afraid to speak evil of dignitaries, ¹¹ whereas angels, who are greater in power and might, do not bring a reviling accusation against them before the Lord.

---

3. Peter has established his apostolic authority and identified himself as an eyewitness to the events in Jesus' life. He will next show why his opponents do not have the same kind of authority . . . and therefore can only be *false* prophets. What does Peter say about the general nature of false prophets? What are their strategies (see verses 1–3)?

_____

_____

_____

_____

_____

_____

_____

_____

4. Peter relates three accounts from the Old Testament to show how God deals with those who despise His authority. The first refers to the angels who rebelled against God in heaven (see Isaiah 14:12–14). The second refers to those destroyed in the Great Flood (see Genesis 6–9). The third describes the fate of the inhabitants of Sodom and

Gomorrah. Whom did God spare in the stories of the Great Flood and the destruction of Sodom and Gomorrah? What conclusions does Peter draw as it relates to God's judgment (see verses 4–11)?

GOING DEEPER

One of the primary problems in the early church was the presence of false teachers who made fine-sounding arguments that led believers astray from the true gospel of Christ. Peter, Paul, and the other apostles frequently had to exert their authority in the Christian communities to show that what they were proclaiming had come from God. In Paul's second letter to Timothy, he emphasizes the message he has proclaimed is come from God and how it can profit a person's life. The writer of Hebrews likewise points out the power of the true gospel and shows that one way to gauge its trustworthiness is to examine its impact on people's lives.

The Man of God and the Word of God (2 Timothy 3:10–17)

[10] But you have carefully followed my doctrine, manner of life, purpose, faith, longsuffering, love, perseverance, [11] persecutions, afflictions, which happened to me at Antioch, at Iconium, at Lystra—what persecutions I endured. And out of them all the Lord delivered me. [12] Yes, and all who desire to live godly in Christ Jesus will suffer persecution. [13] But evil men and impostors will grow worse and worse, deceiving and being deceived. [14] But you must continue in the things which you have learned and been assured of, knowing from whom you have learned them, [15] and that from childhood you have known

the Holy Scriptures, which are able to make you wise for salvation through faith which is in Christ Jesus.

16 All Scripture is given by inspiration of God, and is profitable for doctrine, for reproof, for correction, for instruction in righteousness, 17 that the man of God may be complete, thoroughly equipped for every good work.

5. Paul asks Timothy to recall not only the doctrine he proclaimed but also the example of his life . . . and to expect he will at times also suffer persecution. Some of that persecution was already coming at the hands of "evil men" (obvious enemies of the faith) and "impostors" (those who appear good but work against Christ). How does Paul advise Timothy to combat these individuals? What does he call on Timothy to remember (see verses 10–15)?

_____

_____

_____

_____

_____

_____

6. The phrase "all Scripture" refers not only to the Old Testament but also to the books of the New Testament, some of which had yet to be written. In addition to providing a trustworthy touchstone, how else can God's Word benefit those who embrace it (see verses 16–17)?

_____

_____

_____

_____

_____

The Word Discovers Our Condition (Hebrews 4:11–13)

> [11] Let us therefore be diligent to enter that rest, lest anyone fall according to the same example of disobedience. [12] For the word of God is living and powerful, and sharper than any two-edged sword, piercing even to the division of soul and spirit, and of joints and marrow, and is a discerner of the thoughts and intents of the heart. [13] And there is no creature hidden from His sight, but all things are naked and open to the eyes of Him to whom we must give account.

7. The author of Hebrews points out that God's Word is more than just a historical record of God's work. What descriptive words does he use to emphasize the Bible's potential to impact those who put their trust in its truths and wisdom (see verses 11–12)?

_____

_____

_____

_____

_____

8. Swords and blades are typically viewed as destructive weapons of warfare. However, some blades, such as the surgeon's scalpel, can have a healing effect. What does the trustworthy blade of God's Word do for us? What does it reveal (see verses 12–13)?

_____

_____

_____

_____

_____

REVIEWING THE STORY

Peter defends his apostolic authority and the message he has proclaimed to the believers by reminding them that he was an eyewitness to Jesus' ministry on earth. He states that his words, just like the words of the Old Testament prophets, have been inspired by the Holy Spirit. Peter then addresses his opponents (the false teachers) head-on and exposes their harmful tactics. He states, in no uncertain terms, that God will judge them and those who follow their teaching.

9. What did Peter hear God say when he witnessed the Transfiguration (see 2 Peter 1:17–18)?

_____

_____

_____

_____

_____

10. Why can we trust the prophecy of Scripture (see 2 Peter 1:21)?

_____

_____

_____

_____

_____

11. What warning does Peter give about false teachers in the church (see 2 Peter 2:1–3)?

_____

_____

_____

_____

12. How does Peter characterize those who reject God's authority (see 2 Peter 2:10)?

APPLYING THE MESSAGE

13. What are some of the practices you have employed to ground yourself in God's Word?

14. When has your knowledge of Scripture helped you to discern a false teaching or message?

REFLECTING ON THE MEANING

The passages that we have studied in this section of 2 Peter offer tantalizing evidence to support the Bible's trustworthiness. Many of the writers of Scripture, including Peter, were eyewitnesses to the events they relate. Hundreds of prophecies were fulfilled centuries after they were made. *Everyone* who had a hand in its construction was inspired by the Holy Spirit.

This evidence of the Bible's trustworthiness leads to three important implications for believers. *First, we can learn from the Bible's role models and cautionary tales.* The stories of Joseph and Daniel show us how to please God and build a relationship with Him. The stories of David and Gideon reveals what humility and bold faith look like. At the other end of the scale, the stories of the rebellious angels, the Great Flood, and the destruction of Sodom and Gomorrah provide us with warnings about the dangers of not following God.

Second, we can claim the truths of the Bible for ourselves. If the Bible is trustworthy, there is a lifetime's worth of promises to claim, wisdom to apply, and hope to be received. If we truly prize the truth we find in Scripture—if we regard it as *God's Word*—we will be compelled to do the hard things it says. We will rejoice in the midst of suffering. We will show love to people who hate us. We will place our trust in Jesus' sacrifice to give us eternal life.

Third, we can discover in the Bible how to become spiritually trustworthy ourselves. Peter was able to point out the error in the false teachings that were being proclaimed in the churches because he knew the truth of God's Word. Likewise, when we are grounded in God's Word, we are able to discern the true from the false. There will always be new believers, spiritual seekers, and skeptics looking for answers about Christ—and looking for people to trust with their questions. If we work to grow in our faith through Bible study, prayer, and church involvement, we will gain the trust of these seekers and guide them in their journey.

Peter's words in this section of his letter assure us that the Bible we have received is absolutely truthful. The men who wrote its words were inspired by the Holy Spirit and not just devising cunning fables to trick us. The Word of God can support the full weight of our faith and trust . . . and we will be rewarded when we place our complete faith and trust in it.

JOURNALING YOUR RESPONSE

What are some specific lessons you have learned from the Bible that have shaped your life?

RECOGNIZING FALSE TEACHERS

2 Peter 2:12–22

GETTING STARTED

How do you recognize that something you are hearing is not from God?

SETTING THE STAGE

History reveals that the leaders of the early church had to deal with a number of teachings that ran contrary to gospel of Christ. Today, we would refer to such doctrines as *heresies*. While there were many false teachings in circulation, three of the most prevalent that we find the authors of the New Testament battling were *legalism, antinomianism,* and *gnosticism.* Interestingly, these same false doctrines are prevalent in the church today.

Legalism is the belief that you can earn salvation through good works and by doing your best to follow God's Law (see Ephesians 2:8–9). Antinomianism is the opposite idea—that no rules apply when it comes to the Christian life because we are all saved by God's grace (see Romans 6:1–2). Gnosticism is the belief that you can receive some form of "secret wisdom" outside of the Bible and thus come up with your own rules for living (see Galatians 1:6–7).

Legalism appealed to Jewish Christians who had grown up trying to follow the Law. Antinomianism appealed to Gentile believers who valued personal freedom above all else. Gnosticism appealed to the elite in society who did not like the idea that God saw everyone as equals. Each appealed to one group or another . . . but all led to destruction.

Peter does not identify the specific teachings causing problems in his congregations, but he does indicate the false teachers had arisen from among the community. These were not members of pagan cults but were fellow church members. They knew the Scripture. They had probably heard various Christian evangelists speak. But somewhere along the way, the seed of a wrong idea—a wrong interpretation or way of thinking about the Christian life—had taken root. Like a weed, it had grown into something destructive.

Peter's purpose in this section of his letter is to expose these "weeds"— to call out the depravity of these false teachers with their "great swelling words of emptiness" (2 Peter 2:18). He does not mince words as he denounces their teachings and the way they have misled believers in the congregation. And he leaves no doubt as to the seriousness of their sin.

EXPLORING THE TEXT

Depravity of False Teachers (2 Peter 2:12–17)

¹² But these, like natural brute beasts made to be caught and destroyed, speak evil of the things they do not understand, and will utterly perish in their own corruption, ¹³ and will receive the wages of unrighteousness, as those who count it pleasure to carouse in the daytime. They are spots and blemishes, carousing in their own deceptions while they feast with you, ¹⁴ having eyes full of adultery and that cannot cease from sin, enticing unstable souls. They have a heart trained in covetous practices, and are accursed children. ¹⁵ They have forsaken the right way and gone astray, following the way of Balaam the son of Beor, who loved the wages of unrighteousness; ¹⁶ but he was rebuked for his iniquity: a dumb donkey speaking with a man's voice restrained the madness of the prophet.

¹⁷ These are wells without water, clouds carried by a tempest, for whom is reserved the blackness of darkness forever.

1. Peter states that because these false teachers do their work in the flesh, they are similar to wild animals that are fit only for destruction. What makes these false teachers so useless but also so dangerous (see verses 12–14)?

---

2. In Jewish tradition, the story of Balaam served as a warning against selfishness and greed. He was so intent on cursing the Israelites for his own personal gain that it took a "dumb" animal (a donkey) to restrain him from his madness (see Numbers 22). Peter states the false teachers have followed his ways. What punishment awaited those who seemed to provide spiritual water but ultimately delivered nothing (see verses 15–17)?

_____

_____

_____

_____

_____

_____

_____

_____

Description of False Teachers (2 Peter 2:18–22)

18 For when they speak great swelling words of emptiness, they allure through the lusts of the flesh, through lewdness, the ones who have actually escaped from those who live in error. 19 While they promise them liberty, they themselves are slaves of corruption; for by whom a person is overcome, by him also he is brought into bondage. 20 For if, after they have escaped the pollutions of the world through the knowledge of the Lord and Savior Jesus Christ, they are again entangled in them and overcome, the latter end is worse for them than the beginning. 21 For it would have been better for them not to have known the way of righteousness, than having known it, to turn from the holy commandment delivered to them. 22 But it has happened to them according to the true proverb: "A dog returns to his own vomit," and, "a sow, having washed, to her wallowing in the mire."

3. Peter acknowledges the words of the false teachers—while devoid of any life-giving properties—are nonetheless compelling because they promise liberty without the need to adhere to God's standard of living. But what does Peter say is the reality about this promise of liberty? On what tactics must these teachers rely to lure people in (see verses 18–19)?

_____

_____

_____

_____

_____

_____

_____

4. Peter states that those who are swayed by false teachers after knowing the truth of Christ face more drastic consequences than those who never heard the gospel at all. What images does Peter use to convey the disgusting nature of their decision (see verses 20–22)?

_____

_____

_____

_____

_____

_____

_____

GOING DEEPER

The false teachers in Peter's day were experts at creating doctrines that sounded like the true apostles' teaching but were different in that they appealed to people's greed, lusts, pride, or laziness in doing the hard work it takes to actually follow after God. Like world-class art forgers, the best of them could create counterfeits that *seemed* like the original but were just worthless forgeries. Paul spoke about these practices in his second letter to Timothy and warned about preachers who gave people only the messages they wanted to hear. The disciple John, in his first epistle, likewise urged believers to test every doctrine to make sure it is from God.

Preach the Word (2 Timothy 4:1–5)

¹ I charge you therefore before God and the Lord Jesus Christ, who will judge the living and the dead at His appearing and His kingdom: ² Preach the word! Be ready in season and out of season. Convince, rebuke, exhort, with all longsuffering and teaching. ³ For the time will come when they will not endure sound doctrine, but according to their own desires, because they have itching ears, they will heap up for themselves teachers; ⁴ and they will turn their ears away from the truth, and be turned aside to fables. ⁵ But you be watchful in all things, endure afflictions, do the work of an evangelist, fulfill your ministry.

5. Paul's second letter to Timothy contains thirty-six references to the true gospel and seventeen references to false teachings. What does Paul conclude is the best way for a Christian leader to counteract the influence of false teachers (see verses 1–2)?

6. The phrase "itching ears" refers to those who want to be amused or entertained as opposed to be challenged with God's truth. What happens when teachers give these people what they want (see verses 3–5)?

_____

_____

_____

_____

_____

_____

_____

_____

Love for God and One Another (1 John 4:1–6)

¹ Beloved, do not believe every spirit, but test the spirits, whether they are of God; because many false prophets have gone out into the world. ² By this you know the Spirit of God: Every spirit that confesses that Jesus Christ has come in the flesh is of God, ³ and every spirit that does not confess that Jesus Christ has come in the flesh is not of God. And this is the spirit of the Antichrist, which you have heard was coming, and is now already in the world.

⁴ You are of God, little children, and have overcome them, because He who is in you is greater than he who is in the world. ⁵ They are of the world. Therefore they speak as of the world, and the world hears them. ⁶ We are of God. He who knows God hears us; he who is not of God does not hear us. By this we know the spirit of truth and the spirit of error.

7. John was combating gnostic teachers—those who claimed to have "secret wisdom" from God outside of the true gospel. In this case, the false teachers were claiming to have secret knowledge that Jesus did not take on a physical body while on earth. What strategy does John recommend for spotting false teachings such as this (see verses 1–3)?

_____

_____

_____

_____

_____

8. John states that false teachers have their citizenship in this world, not in heaven, and thus speak the words the world wants to hear. How does that set them apart from true believers? How does it enable true followers of Jesus to recognize their deceptions (see verses 4–6)?

_____

_____

_____

_____

REVIEWING THE STORY

Peter continues to speak out against the false teachers who had arisen in the churches. He refers to them as "brute beasts" who "speak evil of things they do not understand" (2 Peter 2:12). He describes their depravity in leading God's children astray and denounces their self-serving motives. He warns believers that their words are empty and that their promises of liberty will only lead to bondage to sin. Peter is especially appalled that many of these false teachers have come from their own Christian communities. He warns that it would have been better for these individuals to have never encountered the truth of the gospel in the first place.

9. What "wages" will false teachers receive in payment for their misdeeds (see 2 Peter 2:13)?

10. How have false teachers gone "the way of Balaam" (see 2 Peter 2:15–16)?

11. How do false teachers lure in their followers (see 2 Peter 2:18)?

12. What was entangling those false teachers who had received Christ (see 2 Peter 2:20)?

_____

_____

_____

_____

_____

_____

APPLYING THE MESSAGE

13. What are some messages about yourself that the enemy has tried to get you to believe?

_____

_____

_____

_____

_____

_____

14. What methods do you use to "test" whether a message you are hearing is from God?

_____

_____

_____

_____

_____

_____

REFLECTING ON THE MEANING

If it were always easy to spot false teachings, they would not gain much traction in the church. Sadly, many false doctrines contain just enough biblical truth—or what *seems* to be biblical truth—to fly under the radar and start to gain traction. So, this raises the question of how we can *recognize* such false teachings before they take root.

First, we consider the source. Peter states that false teachers are like "wells without water" (2 Peter 2:17). In the world of Peter's day, water from wells was essential to life, and dry wells were quickly identified as being useless in fulfilling their primary purpose. In the same way, we are to consider the "source" of the one doing the teaching and discern whether his or her words are coming from the true "spring of life" that is found only in Christ.

Second, we consider the message. Peter denounced the false teachers of his day as speaking "great swelling words of emptiness" (verse 18). What they had to say was appealing and seemed to be truthful, which enabled them to deceive, entice, and seduce many followers of Christ. Peter was calling his readers to dig deeper into these teachers' messages to get at the heart of what they were actually saying. If the message did not support the truth of the gospel that they had received, they were to reject it as false.

Third, we consult the experts. Remember that Peter began his arguments against the false teachers by first establishing his own credentials. He and the other true apostles were "eyewitnesses of [Christ's] majesty" (1:16). They had walked with Christ, witnessed His miracles, and been with Him after the resurrection. Peter wanted the believers to view him as an expert who would guide them in what was true.

We can do the same today by checking any messages we receive against Scripture to determine whether it aligns with what the Bible says and whether it reflects God's priorities. We can ask God to give us wisdom to discern the difference between His truth and counterfeit teachings. We can also talk to mature believers whose spiritual wisdom we trust to guide us. As we do this, we stamp out any false teaching before it takes root.

JOURNALING YOUR RESPONSE

What is one area in your life today where you need to receive God's wisdom?

STAYING FOCUSED ON HEAVEN

2 Peter 3:1–18

GETTING STARTED

What emotions do you feel when you consider your future in heaven?

_____

_____

_____

_____

_____

_____

_____

_____

_____

_____

_____

_____

SETTING THE STAGE

The doctrines of heaven and Jesus' second coming have traditionally been a cornerstone of Christian theology. But on occasion, some have claimed that the church should instead be focusing on the *important* issues we face on earth. After all, we have all of eternity to learn about heaven! However, if this were true, the authors of the New Testament would not have spent as much time as they do discussing these doctrines. If you removed the information about our future from the Bible, you would remove about one-fourth of its content.

One of the central thoughts in the Bible is that what we think about heaven has a great deal to do with how we live on earth. Heaven is like a tugboat to which we are tied. It pulls us through the present into the future. Peter summarizes this idea in the final section of letter with a piercing question. He writes, "Therefore, since all these things will be dissolved, what manner of persons ought you to be?" (2 Peter 3:11). In other words, in light of God's plan for us in eternity, how are we living our lives for Him in the present?

Peter wanted his readers to recognize they were in a spiritual battle and that they needed to strive for the victory. If they were not careful, they could easily begin to adopt the thinking of this world. They could even end up buying into the lie that this world is all there is—that there is no heaven, no rewards, and no service of God in the new heavens and new earth.

Peter's call is thus for us to stay focused on *heaven*. We are to remember "the day of the Lord will come as a thief in the night" (3:10) and to always be prepared for Jesus' return. This includes partnering with God to rescue as many people as possible from sin, knowing He is "not willing that any should perish but that all should come to repentance" (verse 9). Staying focused on heaven will thus keep us focused on our mission here on this earth.

EXPLORING THE TEXT

God's Promise Is Not Slack (2 Peter 3:1–9)

¹ Beloved, I now write to you this second epistle (in both of which I stir up your pure minds by way of reminder), ² that you may be mindful of the words which were spoken before by the holy prophets, and of the

commandment of us, the apostles of the Lord and Savior, ³knowing this first: that scoffers will come in the last days, walking according to their own lusts, ⁴and saying, "Where is the promise of His coming? For since the fathers fell asleep, all things continue as they were from the beginning of creation." ⁵For this they willfully forget: that by the word of God the heavens were of old, and the earth standing out of water and in the water, ⁶by which the world that then existed perished, being flooded with water. ⁷But the heavens and the earth which are now preserved by the same word, are reserved for fire until the day of judgment and perdition of ungodly men.

⁸But, beloved, do not forget this one thing, that with the Lord one day is as a thousand years, and a thousand years as one day. ⁹The Lord is not slack concerning His promise, as some count slackness, but is longsuffering toward us, not willing that any should perish but that all should come to repentance.

---

1. Peter has spent a large portion of his letter calling out false teachers and warning believers to be wary of their teachings. He now returns to addressing the "beloved," the faithful followers, who evidently were questioning the promise of Jesus' second coming to this earth. What does Peter remind them will happen in the last days? What messages about the events of the future did he want to counteract (see verses 1–6)?

----

2. Peter's point is that what seems like forever to the believers is only a moment for God. What does he say is the cause of God's delay in sending Jesus back (see verses 7–9)?

_____

_____

_____

_____

_____

_____

_____

The Day of the Lord (2 Peter 3:10–18)

¹⁰ But the day of the Lord will come as a thief in the night, in which the heavens will pass away with a great noise, and the elements will melt with fervent heat; both the earth and the works that are in it will be burned up. ¹¹ Therefore, since all these things will be dissolved, what manner of persons ought you to be in holy conduct and godliness, ¹² looking for and hastening the coming of the day of God, because of which the heavens will be dissolved, being on fire, and the elements will melt with fervent heat? ¹³ Nevertheless we, according to His promise, look for new heavens and a new earth in which righteousness dwells.

¹⁴ Therefore, beloved, looking forward to these things, be diligent to be found by Him in peace, without spot and blameless; ¹⁵ and consider that the longsuffering of our Lord is salvation—as also our beloved brother Paul, according to the wisdom given to him, has written to you, ¹⁶ as also in all his epistles, speaking in them of these things, in which are some things hard to understand, which untaught and unstable people twist to their own destruction, as they do also the rest of the Scriptures.

[17] You therefore, beloved, since you know this beforehand, beware lest you also fall from your own steadfastness, being led away with the error of the wicked; [18] but grow in the grace and knowledge of our Lord and Savior Jesus Christ.

To Him be the glory both now and forever. Amen.

---

3. The "day of the Lord" refers to Jesus' second coming, His judgment of the earth, and the coming of the new heavens and new earth. Peter states that this day will arrive "as a thief in the night" and that it will be accompanied by cataclysmic events. What does Peter ask his readers to consider as it relates to their conduct in light of these coming events (see verses 10–13)?

_____

_____

_____

_____

_____

_____

4. Peter closes with three commands for his readers: (1) look forward to these events, (2) be diligent in leading a godly life, and (3) continue to persevere in spite of suffering (see verses 14–15). What ultimately will set them apart from "untaught and unstable people" (verse 16)? Of what should they beware as they look forward to Jesus' return (see verses 17–18)?

_____

_____

_____

_____

_____

GOING DEEPER

As Peter closes his second letter, he urges his readers to continue living in expectation of Jesus' return and to continue diligently pursuing those tasks that God has called them to fulfill. The apostle Paul, in his letter to the Colossians, likewise encouraged believers to keep living with a focus on heaven and set their minds on things above. The disciple John, in his first epistle, also asks his readers to keep their focus on heaven by not loving the things of this world.

Not Carnality but Christ (Colossians 3:1–7)

¹ If then you were raised with Christ, seek those things which are above, where Christ is, sitting at the right hand of God. ² Set your mind on things above, not on things on the earth. ³ For you died, and your life is hidden with Christ in God. ⁴ When Christ who is our life appears, then you also will appear with Him in glory.

⁵ Therefore put to death your members which are on the earth: fornication, uncleanness, passion, evil desire, and covetousness, which is idolatry. ⁶ Because of these things the wrath of God is coming upon the sons of disobedience, ⁷ in which you yourselves once walked when you lived in them.

5. Right now, Jesus is in heaven, sitting at the right hand of God. If we are "raised with Christ" and our "life is hidden with Christ," where should our thoughts be (see verses 1–4)?

_____

_____

_____

_____

_____

_____

6. Paul states there are certain things we need to "put to death" in our lives. What needs to be put to death so we can maintain our focus on things above (see verses 5–7)?

_____

_____

_____

_____

_____

_____

_____

Do Not Love the World (1 John 2:15–17)

> [15] Do not love the world or the things in the world. If anyone loves the world, the love of the Father is not in him. [16] For all that is in the world—the lust of the flesh, the lust of the eyes, and the pride of life—is not of the Father but is of the world. [17] And the world is passing away, and the lust of it; but he who does the will of God abides forever.

7. When John mentions "the world" in this passage, he is referring to the whole of sinful humanity. What happens when we choose to love the world (see verse 15)?

_____

_____

_____

_____

_____

8. John writes that the things of the world—"the lust of the flesh, the lust of the eyes, and the pride of life" (verse 16)—are not of God. What else does John say about loving these things? Why is doing God's will a better investment of our time (see verses 16–17)?

_____

_____

_____

_____

_____

REVIEWING THE STORY

Peter closes his second letter by calling the believers to remember the words of God's prophets and avoid "scoffers" who will say He will not fulfill His promise of sending Jesus back to this world. He tells them that God's timetable for Jesus' return is different from any person's on earth. In the meantime, they are to live in expectation of His return as "a thief in the night," look forward to the day when God will judge all unrighteousness, and keep pursuing the godly life that God desires. Peter ends with a final warning for the believers to avoid those who seek to lead them astray and to continue to grow in the knowledge of their Lord and Savior.

9. What did Peter want to "stir up" in writing his letters (see 2 Peter 3:1)?

_____

_____

_____

_____

_____

10. What does Peter remind his readers once happened to this world (see 2 Peter 3:6)?

_____

_____

_____

_____

_____

_____

_____

_____

11. How does Peter describe the day of the Lord (see 2 Peter 3:10–11)?

_____

_____

_____

_____

_____

_____

_____

_____

12. What does Peter say that some people had tried to do with Scripture (see 2 Peter 3:16)?

_____

_____

_____

_____

_____

_____

APPLYING THE MESSAGE

13. How do you respond to those who scoff at the promise that Jesus will return to this world?

_____

_____

_____

_____

_____

_____

_____

_____

14. What does it mean for you to go through each day with your focus fixed on heaven?

_____

_____

_____

_____

_____

_____

_____

REFLECTING ON THE MEANING

Peter notes in this final section of his letter that scoffers will come in the last days and mock the promise of Jesus' return. However, they forget that God operates according to His own timetable. He fulfilled all the prophecies in the Old Testament about Christ's first coming, and we can be sure that He will fulfill all the prophecies concerning Jesus' second coming.

In the meantime, there are three things we must be tough-minded to do as we focus on our future.

First, we must stay tough-minded about our purpose. As we look to the coming of Christ, we must "be diligent to be found by Him in peace, without spot and blameless" (verse 14). God has provided us with specific spiritual gifts so that we can serve in the body of Christ and accomplish the good works that He wants us to do in this world. It can be tempting at times to just lapse into apathy, but we must remember that one day we will stand before Christ and give an account of what we have not done (or not done) for Him.

Second, we must be tough-minded about our profession. Peter warns about "untaught and unstable people" who will try to twist the words of the Bible to their own advantage (2 Peter 3:16). For this reason, we need to know what we believe and be able to back it up with the truths found in Scripture. This way, when people come to our door peddling a heretical view of Christ, we can remain steadfast in our convictions and not be swayed by their words. We must stand firm in our profession and our confession of our faith in Jesus.

Third, we must be tough-minded about our progress. Peter exhorts us to "grow in the grace and knowledge of our Lord and Savior Jesus Christ" (verse 18). We grow when we abide in God's will. We grow when we choose to get down on our knees and meet with God in prayer. We grow by studying the God's Word. And we grow through our service to His church. God designed us to grow together, so we must be tough-minded about being in church, small groups, and other settings where we can be sharpened, inspired, and encouraged by others.

The noted theologian C.S. Lewis once said that when we look at the testimony of history, we find that the Christians who did the most for this present world were those who were most focused on the next one. Keeping our focus on heaven enables us to not only *survive* in this world but also to *thrive*. When we become more heavenly minded, we make ourselves available for God to use us to do more earthly good than we ever thought possible.

Journaling Your Response

What are you seeking to do each day to grow just a bit more in your spiritual life?

LEADER'S GUIDE

Thank you for choosing to lead your group through this study from Dr. David Jeremiah on *The Letters of 1 and 2 Peter*. Being a group leader has its own rewards, and it is our prayer that your walk with the Lord will deepen through this experience. During the twelve lessons in this study, you and your group will read selected passages from 1 and 2 Peter, explore key themes in the letter based on teachings from Dr. Jeremiah, and review questions that will encourage group discussion. There are multiple components in this section that can help you structure your lessons and discussion time, so please be sure to read and consider each one.

BEFORE YOU BEGIN

Before your first meeting, make sure you and your group are well versed with the content of the lesson. Group members should have their own copy of *The Letters of 1 and 2 Peter* study guide prior to the first meeting so they can follow along and record their answers, thoughts, and insights. After the first week, you may wish to assign the study guide lesson as homework prior to the group meeting and then use the meeting time to discuss the content in the lesson.

To ensure everyone has a chance to participate in the discussion, the ideal size for a group is around eight to ten people. If there are more than ten people, break up the bigger group into smaller subgroups. Make sure the members are committed to participating each week, as this will help create stability and help you better prepare the structure of the meeting.

At the beginning of each week's study, start with the opening Getting Started question to introduce the topic you will be discussing. The members should answer briefly, as the goal is just for them to have an idea of the subject in their minds as you go over the lesson. This will allow the members to become engaged and ready to interact with the rest of the group.

After reviewing the lesson, try to initiate a free-flowing discussion. Invite group members to bring questions and insights they may have discovered to the next meeting, especially if they were unsure of the meaning of some parts of the lesson. Be prepared to discuss how biblical truth applies to the world we live in today.

WEEKLY PREPARATION

As the group leader, here are a few things that you can do to prepare for each meeting:

- *Be thoroughly familiar with the material in the lesson.* Make sure that you understand the content of each lesson so you know how to structure the group time and are prepared to lead the group discussion.

- *Decide, ahead of time, which questions you want to discuss.* Depending on how much time you have each week, you may not be able to reflect on every question. Select specific questions that you feel will evoke the best discussion.

- *Take prayer requests.* At the end of your discussion, take prayer requests from your group members and then pray for one another.

STRUCTURING THE DISCUSSION TIME

There are several ways to structure the duration of the study. You can choose to cover each lesson individually, for a total of twelve weeks of group meetings, or you can combine two lessons together per week, for a total of six weeks of group meetings. The following charts illustrate these options:

TWELVE-WEEK FORMAT

Week	Lessons Covered	Reading
1	A Living Hope	1 Peter 1:1–12
2	Pursuing Holiness	1 Peter 1:13–25
3	Pursuing Spiritual Growth	1 Peter 2:1–12
4	Submitting to Authority	1 Peter 2:13–25
5	Submitting in the Home	1 Peter 3:1–12
6	Suffering in This World	1 Peter 3:13–22
7	Adopting the Mind of Christ	1 Peter 4:1–19
8	Combating the Enemy	1 Peter 5:1–14
9	Leading an Exceptional Life	2 Peter 1:1–15
10	Embracing the Truth	2 Peter 1:16–2:11
11	Recognizing False Teachers	2 Peter 2:12–22
12	Staying Focused on Heaven	2 Peter 3:1–18

SIX-WEEK FORMAT

Week	Lessons Covered	Reading
1	A Living Hope / Pursuing Holiness	1 Peter 1:1–25
2	Pursuing Spiritual Growth / Submitting to Authority	1 Peter 2:1–25
3	Submitting in the Home / Suffering in This World	1 Peter 3:1–22
4	Adopting the Mind of Christ / Combating the Enemy	1 Peter 4:1–5:14
5	Leading an Exceptional Life / Embracing the Truth	2 Peter 1:1–2:11
6	Recognizing False Teachers / Staying Focused on Heaven	2 Peter 2:12–3:18

In regard to organizing your time when planning your group Bible study, the following two schedules, for sixty minutes and ninety minutes, can give you a structure for the lesson:

Section	60 Minutes	90 Minutes
Welcome: Members arrive and get settled	5 minutes	10 minutes
Getting Started Question: Prepares the group for interacting with one another	10 minutes	10 minutes
Message: Review the lesson	15 minutes	25 minutes
Discussion: Discuss questions in the lesson	25 minutes	35 minutes
Review and Prayer: Review the key points of the lesson and have a closing time of prayer	5 minutes	10 minutes

As the group leader, it is up to you to keep track of the time and keep things moving according to your schedule. If your group is having a good discussion, don't feel the need to stop and move on to the next question. Remember, the purpose is to pull together ideas and share unique insights on the lesson. Encourage everyone to participate, but don't be concerned if certain group members are more quiet. They may just be internally reflecting on the questions and need time to process their ideas before they can share them.

GROUP DYNAMICS

Leading a group study can be a rewarding experience for you and your group members—but that doesn't mean there won't be challenges. Certain members may feel uncomfortable discussing topics that they consider very personal and might be afraid of being called on. Some members might have disagreements on specific issues. To help prevent these scenarios, consider the following ground rules:

- If someone has a question that may seem off topic, suggest that it be discussed at another time, or ask the group if they are okay with addressing that topic.

- If someone asks a question you don't know the answer to, confess that you don't know and move on. If you feel comfortable, invite other group members to give their opinions or share their comments based on personal experience.
- If you feel like a couple of people are talking much more than others, direct questions to people who may not have shared yet. You could even ask the more dominating members to help draw out the quiet ones.
- When there is a disagreement, encourage the group members to process the matter in love. Invite members from opposing sides to evaluate their opinions and consider the ideas of the other members. Lead the group through Scripture that addresses the topic, and look for common ground.

When issues arise, encourage your group to think of Scripture: "Love one another" (John 13:34), "If it is possible, as much as it depends on you, live peaceably with all men" (Romans 12:18), and, "Be swift to hear, slow to speak, slow to wrath" (James 1:19).

ABOUT

Dr. David Jeremiah and Turning Point

Dr. David Jeremiah is the founder of Turning Point, a ministry committed to providing Christians with sound Bible teaching relevant to today's changing times through radio and television broadcasts, audio series, books, and live events. Dr. Jeremiah's teaching on topics such as family, prayer, worship, angels, and biblical prophecy forms the foundation of Turning Point.

David and his wife, Donna, reside in El Cajon, California, where he serves as the senior pastor of Shadow Mountain Community Church. David and Donna have four children and twelve grandchildren.

In 1982, Dr. Jeremiah brought the same solid teaching to San Diego television that he shares weekly with his congregation. Shortly thereafter, Turning Point expanded its ministry to radio. Dr. Jeremiah's inspiring messages can now be heard worldwide on radio, television, and the internet.

Because Dr. Jeremiah desires to know his listening audience, he travels nationwide holding ministry rallies and spiritual enrichment conferences that touch the hearts and lives of many people. According to Dr. Jeremiah, "At some point in time, everyone reaches a turning point; and for every person, that moment is unique, an experience to hold onto forever. There's so much changing in today's world that sometimes it's difficult to choose the right path. Turning Point offers people an understanding of God's Word and seeks to make a difference in their lives."

Dr. Jeremiah has authored numerous books, including *Escape the Coming Night* (Revelation), *The Handwriting on the Wall* (Daniel), *What in the World Is Going On?*, *The Coming Economic Armageddon*, *I Never Thought I'd See the Day!*, *God Loves You: He Always Has—He Always Will*, *Agents of the Apocalypse*, *Agents of Babylon*, *Revealing the Mysteries of Heaven*, *People Are Asking . . . Is This the End?*, *A Life Beyond Amazing*, *Overcomer*, *The Book of Signs*, *Everything You Need*, *Forward*, and *Where Do We Go from Here?*

STAY CONNECTED
to Dr. David Jeremiah

Take advantage of two great ways to let Dr. David Jeremiah give you spiritual direction every day!

Turning Points Magazine and Devotional

Receive Dr. David Jeremiah's magazine, *Turning Points*, each month and discover:

- Thematic study focus
- 48 pages of life-changing reading
- Relevant articles
- Special features
- Daily devotional readings
- Bible study resource offers
- Live event schedule
- Radio & television information

Request *Turning Points* magazine today!

(800) 947-1993
www.DavidJeremiah.org/Magazine

Daily Turning Point E-Devotional

Start your day off right! Find words of inspiration and spiritual motivation waiting for you on your computer every morning! Receive a daily e-devotion communication from David Jeremiah that will strengthen your walk with God and encourage you to live the authentic Christian life.

Request your free e-devotional today!

(800) 947-1993
www.DavidJeremiah.org/Devo

New Bible Study Series
from Dr. David Jeremiah

The Jeremiah Bible Study Series captures Dr. David Jeremiah's forty-plus years of commitment to teaching the whole Word of God. Each volume contains twelve lessons for individuals and groups to explore what the Bible says, what it meant to the people at the time it was written, and what it means to us today. Out of his lifelong ministry of *delivering the unchanging Word of God to an ever-changing world*, Dr. Jeremiah has written this Bible-strong study series focused not on causes, current events, or politics, but on the solid truth of Scripture.

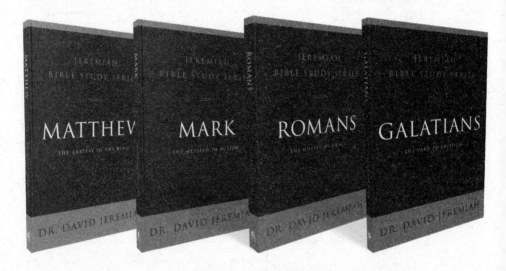